THE MEANING OF
WOOF

CONTENTS

PART 1

A BEAUTIFUL FRIENDSHIP

Humans and dogs have forged a mutual bond
of love and respect that has lasted thousands of years.

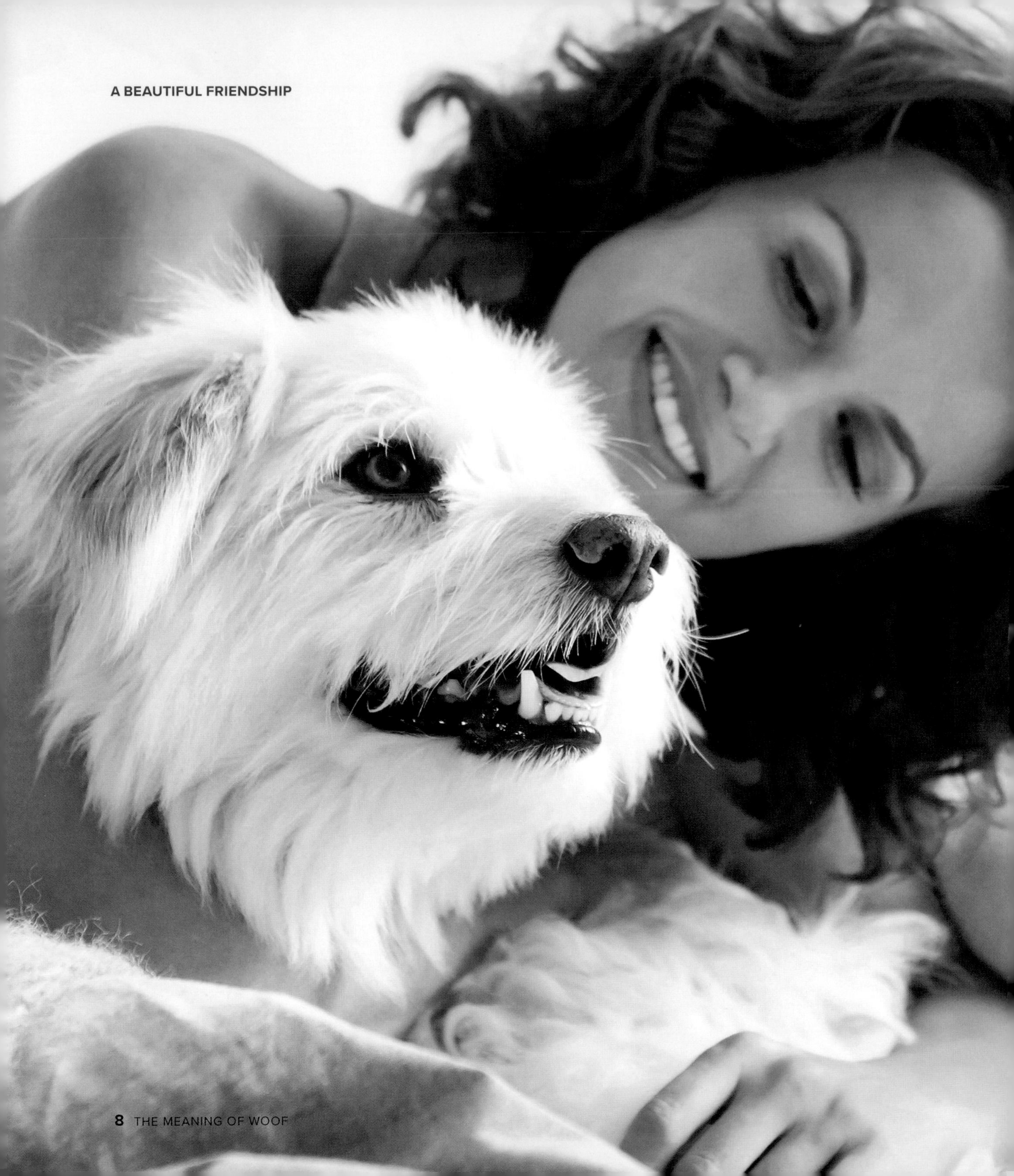

WHY WE LOVE DOGS (AND THEY LOVE US)

From the earliest time of hunter-gatherers and wolves, dogs and humans have shared a special bond that's still going strong today.

They are always excited to see you when you walk through the door. They comfort you when you're sad. They're the best listeners and will never judge or spill your secrets. They love you unconditionally. These are just a few qualities that have earned dogs the title of man's best friend (a term that reportedly dates back to Frederick the Great of Prussia in the mid-18th century), and given dogs around the globe a special place in our hearts and homes.

While the exact origin of the human-dog relationship is still debated, it likely began many thousands of years ago (scientists say anywhere from 20,000 to 40,000), when wolves began to scrounge around nomadic hunter-gatherer camps, looking for scraps and leftovers. The ones who were more sociable and less aggressive succeeded best—and over time, these animals evolved to resemble at least a little more closely the family-friendly Fidos we know and love today. Dogs, in fact, were the first animals to be domesticated, and eventually they became part of the workforce, helping with a range of responsibilities, from guarding to herding to hunting.

Plenty of dogs still earn their keep—assisting people with disabilities; aiding in search-and-rescue operations; providing therapy; racing sleds; sniffing out illicit goods and bombs; and preening at dog shows. But many more are not just our pets—they are beloved family members with an unbreakable bond with us.

In fact, a true emotional connection occurs when dogs and people look at each other, according to a 2015 study published in the journal *Science*. The research discovered that after humans and dogs looked into one another's eyes during a 30-minute period, oxytocin, aka the "love hormone," increased in both parties. (Oxytocin is also released when mothers connect with their newborn babies.) Another study, published in the journal *Cell*, revealed that dogs can read human facial expressions and make decisions based on them, proving that they have a high level of emotional intelligence. Need proof? Simply look at your dog, without saying anything, and smile—you'll likely get a tail wag in return. That's why dogs are more likely to listen to you when you look happy and why the way you interact with your dog has a major impact on his behavior.

FORGING BONDS

So why is there such a strong connection between people and their dogs? Some experts say it came out of our mutual courtship. "I think it's so successful because it came organically, rather than one pushing the other into it," notes Jessica Oliva, PhD, an instructor in the School of Psychological Sciences at Monash University in Melbourne, Australia, who began studying the role of oxytocin in human and dog interactions after adopting her own pooch from an animal-rescue shelter. "The bond that followed was my inspiration to carry out my research. I wanted to quantify it in some way. But what I learned is, you can't measure that love—it transcends anything that can be measured with science. It's something you can learn only through experience."

Still, science does seem to make a point. Oliva's research implicates the oxytocin receptor gene in the evolution from wolf to domesticated dog and suggests that changes in this system are at least partly the reason that, as a species, dogs are able to form strong emotional bonds with humans. But exactly what those changes are remains unknown. It's possible that the oxytocin receptor distribution in dogs' brains has changed, making them more open to the interspecies bonding that exists between humans and canines. "Of course, some dogs are simply more aloof than others," notes Oliva. "There could be a lot of reasons behind this: breed, early environment, attachment style of their owner, or genetic differences."

STRENGTHENING TIES

Clearly, though, the relationship is not a balanced one. We are the ones holding the leash, and we need to be careful not to exploit our relationship with our dogs, adds Oliva. "We definitely have the power, but should remain humble, because while dogs have evolved to understand and use our communication signals—such as following verbal and nonverbal human commands like pointing—

> Research has found that when humans and their dogs maintain eye contact, both show boosted levels of the "love hormone," oxytocin.

Don't underestimate your dog's ability to read—and react to—your facial expressions.

we haven't evolved the reciprocal abilities. For example, we don't understand what a dog is saying when it barks." That's why studying and understanding more about animal cognition and emotion is so important and can help to give animals a voice, she notes.

So just like you want your dog to pay attention when you ask her to sit or stay, so should you be more aware of what your animal is trying to tell you, says Oliva. "We need to be able to see our dog for what it is: a dog. And we need to sit back and look at how our own behaviors and emotions might be influencing our dogs' actions." In other words, while dogs are often highly attuned to how we're feeling, we don't always take a moment to do the same for them.

To be your dog's best friend in the right way, study his cues for information on his emotional state. "Lots of people treat them like human babies, focusing on fulfilling a deep desire they have for unconditional love and affection—which gives the human a great deal of satisfaction, but doesn't necessarily do much to help the dog," says Oliva. (People who dress up their dogs in tutus and sunglasses, we're talking to you.) "When you really care for a dog, without wanting anything in return, or you make some sacrifices from your own life when necessary—that's when you really experience love." ❧

60.2 million
Number of U.S. households with a dog

Strengthen your connection with your dog by working to stay attuned to his feelings.

Spending time
with a dog
can fight stress,
anxiety, depression
and more.

HOME

ALL IN THE FAMILY

Why (almost) everyone should have a dog.

 et's get real: Nobody needs a dog. They chew your children's toys or, worse, your shoes. They steal the rib roast off the counter, then hog the sofa. They shed or need to be routinely groomed—or both. They bark while the baby naps and when the boss calls. They exert special forces over which you have little control, like when you dip into your wallet at the pet store and impulse-buy a stuffed hedgehog because it not only squeaks, it snorts. And you don't possess the strength to stand between your last $20 and a squeaky-snorty hedgehog.

Given all the reasons not to have a dog, how can you explain how much a dog means to someone who's never owned one and feels nothing for them? Love for a dog, as any dog owner knows, defies logic and knows no boundaries. I mean, would you crouch to the ground with a plastic bag over your hand to pick up a friend's poop? I'm thinking...no.

Practically speaking, it didn't make sense for our family to get a dog when we did. I don't have a fenced yard (which, if you know dogs and their early wake-up bathroom calls, is highly convenient). I have three kids, all of whom require attention, particularly the youngest. Besides, it was summer, with lazy seaside days beckoning and no worries about packing up the beach blanket early to get home to walk the dog. "You don't want a dog, not now," said my best friend.

Oh, but I did. And as soon as I saw him, I knew.

We'd had a dog who'd lived to a ripe old age, so I knew firsthand about children's overly ambitious promises to walk him. And we knew the worst part about having a pet: the sorrow of saying our final goodbyes and the void afterward. Nearly a year had gone by since our beloved pointer died when a video of a floppy-eared dog popped up in my news feed. I watched it, over and over, then sent it to my husband with a seemingly innocuous comment. "Cute, isn't he?" I expected my practical husband to talk me down or at least remind me of our current freedom from having to take care of a dog. Instead, he had the same reaction I did: What a great-looking dog. Crap.

I called the rescue, the same one that we adopted our first dog from, and made an appointment to meet the dog with his foster mom at a park. I took my teenage

Your new dog might not bond immediately with you—but once he does, it's for life.

son with me, and we met Charlie. Black and white, with a beautiful spotted coat and a stubby, mutilated tail that sadly betrayed abuse in his young life, Charlie was smaller in person and cowered in our presence. He was reportedly very food-motivated but shied away from our treats. He was 2, yet he had no concept of walking on a leash, circling and tangling up anyone who tried. He'd had a rough start—and, naturally, it showed.

"He's not perfect," his foster mom said. Feeling sympathy and trepidation all at once, I felt the rush of a project with potential—like some of the guys I'd dated in my 20s, only with likelier odds of success.

Since I'd had conversations with Charlie's foster mom before our visit, I believed her when she ticked off his attributes: that he was a cuddler, loved to play and liked kids. Charlie finally looked up at my son with soft brown eyes and relaxed long enough to enjoy some bonding time on a short, impossible walk. It was a done deal. We exchanged the paperwork, thanked his foster mom and brought Charlie home.

As much as we knew we wanted Charlie, he wasn't so sold on us. We expected him to be wary, and he spent his first day in his new forever home nervously glued upright to our couch. We gave him time, food and our compassion, and over the coming days and weeks, not only did Charlie come around, but he grew extraordinarily

Most dogs enjoy being petted on the chest and shoulders.

A BEAUTIFUL FRIENDSHIP

Many dogs will be friendly to everyone in the household, but will also have a special human.

> **Studies show that some dogs will immediately feel at home with you once they realize you are the source of their food. Others need a bit more time.**

affectionate. He's a 36-pound lap dog who loves to give kisses, play fetch and paw us for attention.

Now that Charlie's been with us a few months, all I can think about is how empty our house seemed before he joined our family. I have two teenagers, and while they don't care to, say, have their parents cuddle them much anymore, it's a peaceful feeling to see them with Charlie curled close by their side while they climb their mountains of homework. With teenage hormones taking over the house, the dog is Switzerland, a neutral party everyone adores. He's always there with his sweet, no-judgment-zone face, which eases everyone's stress. (I'd argue that if you have teens, you absolutely need a dog. Who else is going to run to the door to greet you?) My first-grader loves Charlie for his pure cuteness and helps to feed and walk him. Learning early to care for her fellow creatures is a nice bonus lesson.

What's more, we know our neighbors from our thrice-daily walks, especially our neighbors with dogs. Before the family a few doors away got a dog, our relationship was pretty much a series of cordial hellos and

goodbyes. Now that their pup and Charlie are pals, we watch them play while we talk about our kids, the neighborhood and the crazy trudge toward college. Another new neighbor couple, much younger and without kids—people we might not otherwise see much because we move in different circles—have a puppy, and our dogs have romped around while we talk and get to know one another. Dogs bring people, and communities, closer together.

As for Charlie, I'd be lying if I said life with a dog is ideal. He's an adept toy thief and slayer of stuffed animals, but at least that encourages cleaning up and decluttering. He has his quirks— like being choosy about who gets to walk him, depending on who's home. One of his favorite cozy spots is directly under my bed, and he's woken my husband and me in the middle of the night with his digging to nowhere. One night, we heard him helping himself to a long drink—from the toilet bowl. Dogs are a little disgusting, but when they love you and your family no matter what, who cares? He's not perfect. And we wouldn't trade him for anything. —*Gail O'Connor* 🐾

Despite their common ancestry, dogs and wolves evolved on very different paths.

HOW DOGS BECAME PETS

Scientists have differing theories for how man's best friend evolved from a wild wolf to a domesticated dog.

The true history of how wild wolves evolved into domesticated pets is as mysterious as what our dogs do all day while we're at work. Scientists have plenty of theories, but they can't seem to agree on a few of the core aspects—like how long ago the evolution began and where in the world it first occurred. But one thing is certain: Over the course of thousands of years, the body and temperament of the white wolf changed— its skull, teeth and paws shrank, and its disposition became docile the more it interacted with humans. In recent centuries, we refined the species with selective breeding, resulting in the hundreds of dog breeds in existence.

Depending on the scientific study, DNA analysis of dog fossils suggests they were wild anywhere from 12,000 to 130,000 years ago. But in 2017, Krishna R. Veeramah, PhD, assistant professor of ecology and evolution at New York's Stony Brook University, and his team narrowed down the window considerably. Analyzing two prehistoric dogs from Germany, they found evidence that domestication first began between 20,000 and 40,000 years ago.

Genetics studies have cited everywhere from Europe, Central Asia, South Asia and the Middle East as possible origins for that domestication. There's also the question of whether the event happened once or twice—which might explain why the Chihuahua and the bulldog don't even look like the same species. Some scientists believe domestication first began in Asia and that some time after, their lineages split into East Asian and Western Eurasian dogs. Similarly, Veeramah's team found evidence of a 5,000-year-old canine to be a mixture of European dogs and current central Asian/Indian dogs, which could suggest that people who moved into Europe from the Eurasian steppes at the beginning of the Bronze

Age (circa 4000 B.C.) brought their own dogs with them. According to Veeramah, "There was likely only a single domestication event for the dogs observed in the fossil record from the Stone Age and that we also see and live with today."

Other researchers think there was domestication twice, both in Western and Eastern Eurasia, and that the Western version didn't survive. An Oxford University study suggests the presence of older fossils in Europe and Asia and the lack of dogs older than 8,000 years in between those regions supports that theory. "Maybe the reason there hasn't yet been a consensus about where dogs were domesticated is because everyone has been a little bit right," says Greg Larson, director of Oxford University's Palaeogenomics and Bio-Archaeology Research Network.

There's also the question of why wolves were domesticated in the first place. And just like the others, it remains unanswered, as experts hold varying theories. Some think early humans captured wolf pups and kept them as pets. Others suggest it was the wolf that ingratiated itself to get out of the cold and into warm homes. Once domesticated, wolves served different functions, depending on the region. In Siberia, they were sled dogs (an early version of the Siberian husky) and would pull owners across rough terrain. In Asia, they were hunting partners used to track and retrieve wounded game in densely wooded forests. These dogs were so revered, early records indicate

some were named, considered family members and even buried with grave markers. Similar proper burials have also been discovered in the regions of Europe and North America.

Fast-forward thousands of years, and the history of the dog firms up. Over the past few centuries, dogs have evolved into the many diverse breeds we know and love today. Due to artificial selection by humans, the animal's brain, behaviors and genetics have also been modified to make the dog sort of the perfect companion. "The way the game works is very simple," explains animal psychologist Stanley Coren, PhD. "You have a dog, and that dog is very friendly. So that dog is more apt to get better care and better food, and that's the one you want to breed. Over generations, you end up with a dog who not only is friendly but can communicate better with people. For example, if I point to something, my dog knows I'm indicating that in the direction I'm pointing is something of interest, and the dog will usually go over in that particular direction. A wolf will not. If you point, a wolf will look at your hand, not in the direction you're pointing, and that's even if it's a wolf who has been reared from puppyhood in a human family. So the genetics have actually

changed. The genetic ability to recognize communications signals has been changed. Dogs have been modified to be our companions."

Another example of the vast difference between wolves and modern dogs is their diet. Some experts say canines should be fed a raw diet, since they're "basically just tame wolves," adds Coren. "That's a bunch of nonsense. Dogs are thousands of generations different from tame wolves, and a typical example is the fact that a wolf is basically an obligatory carnivore. It's got, maybe, two of the anomalous protein genes that will allow it to eat carbohydrates—which isn't much, so it gets sick. On the other hand, the domestic dog can have up to 40 of those genes. He's adapted, so he will be able to eat that pizza crust you're offering him as a treat, because he's living in the niche where human beings live—and we eat a lot of carbohydrates."

Regardless of when and where wolves were first domesticated, one thing is certain: Canines wouldn't be here today without us. And because of that timeless bond, the two species have forged a deep relationship based on mutual love and fondness. "God may have created man," notes Coren, "but man created dog." ❧

> ## Wolves and dogs are genetically related, but their differing behaviors show the effects of centuries of domestication.

Canines are the first species (and only large carnivore) to have been domesticated.

Children learn
empathy from
living with
and caring for
a family pet.

A
14,000-year-
old grave of a
man, woman and
dog in Germany is
the earliest
evidence of
human-pet
bonding.

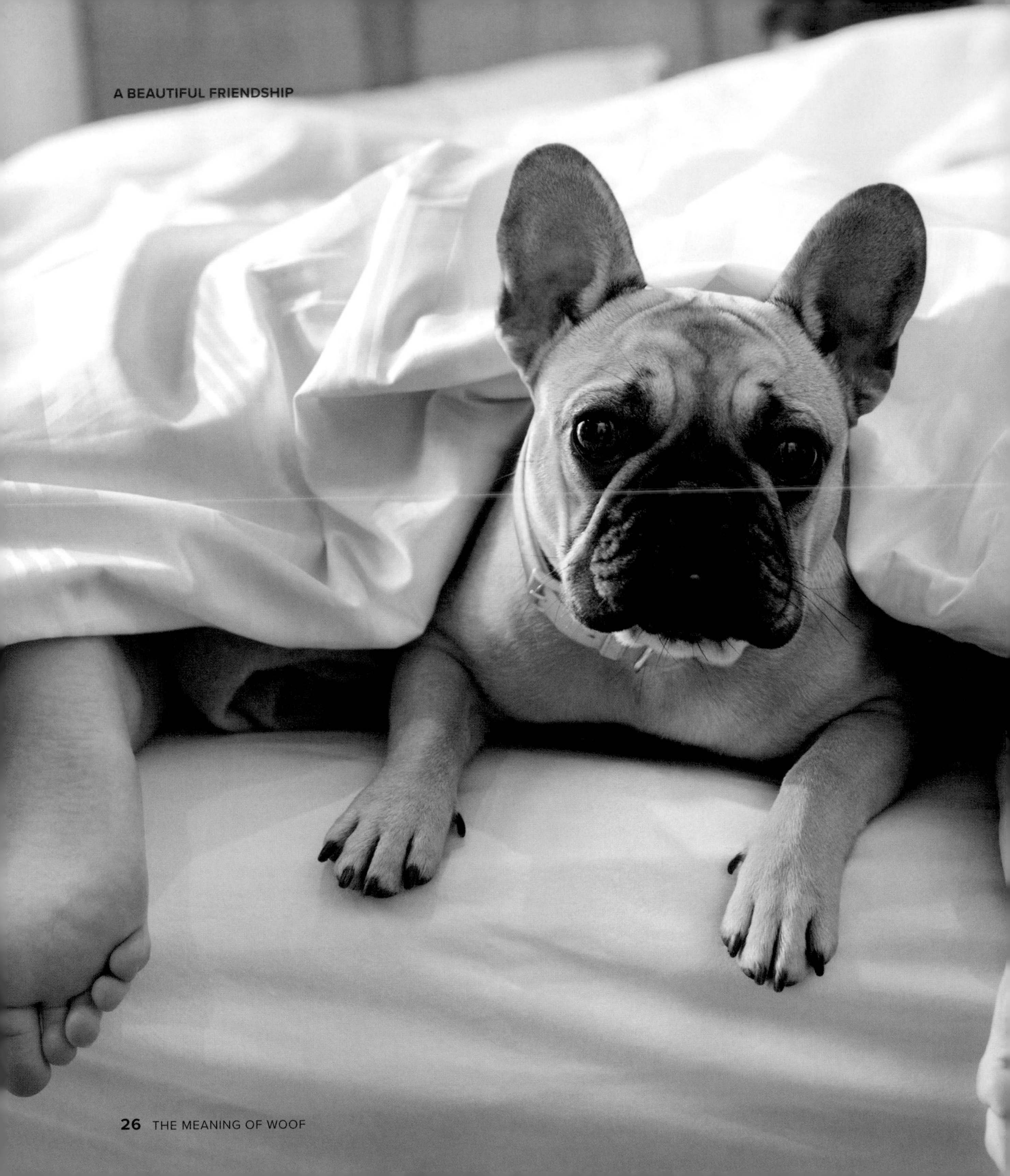

Health Benefits of Owning a Dog

WHEN YOU OPEN UP YOUR HOME to a dog, you're doing more than saving its life. Zooeyia, the idea that pets are good for human health, is believed to benefit us physically, mentally and emotionally. Whether it's taking your dog on daily walks or cuddling with her, "the positive health effects associated with an affectionate relationship with a pet include reduced cardiovascular disease risk, lowered blood pressure, lower cholesterol, stress reduction, better surgical recovery rates and lower incidence of loneliness and depression, among other things," explains psychologist and sociologist Lisa F. Carver, PhD. Getting out of the house to walk your dog or take it to the park doesn't just provide physical activity but can also help alleviate isolation, improve your social life and increase human-human interaction.

And it's not just adults who benefit from a four-legged pal. "Research has shown that children who own dogs are significantly more empathetic than those who own cats," adds Carver. "There has been some evidence to suggest it is the dog's ability to demonstrate affection for children and to pay attention to them that assists in the development of empathy. Dogs will greet children enthusiastically, seek them out to play and provide companionship and affection. In single-parent families, this attachment between children and their dogs can be especially important."

DID YOU KNOW

5 FUN FACTS ABOUT DOGS

Seeing the world through your pet's eyes requires an intuitive mentality.

THEY SEE REALLY WELL AT NIGHT

Your dog has a lot better chance than you of spotting something lurking in the shadows, thanks to adaptations that boost his vision when it's dark. That includes larger pupils and more light-sensitive cells in the center of the retina that work better in dim light. He also has a special mirror-like membrane that reflects light and gives the retina an additional chance to register light. (It's also what causes your dog's eyes to glow at night.)

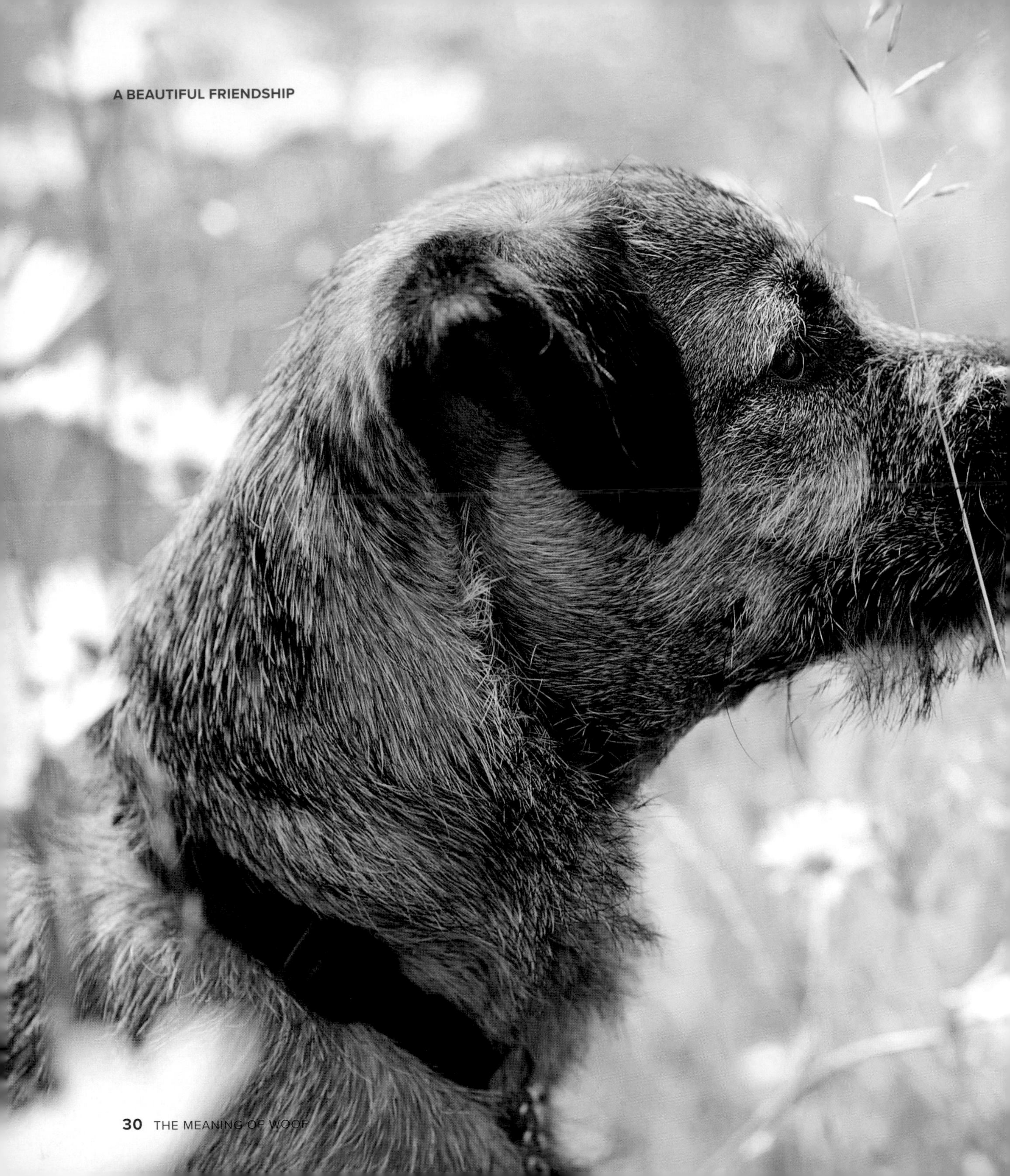

When a dog sniffs, the air goes down two separate paths: some to its lungs, and some to its scent detectors.

SHE REALLY DOESN'T LIKE IT WHEN YOU YELL

Puppies are born deaf, but that changes quickly. Within a month, dogs can hear at four times the distance as humans. They can also register high-pitched sounds with frequency ranges up to 45,000 Hz—we hear between 20 Hz and 20,000 Hz—which is why loud noises can be so uncomfortable to them.

Dogs may tilt their heads or move their ears to better direct sounds to their ears.

THEY LOVE IT WHEN YOU COOK DINNER

A dog's sense of smell is 10,000 to 100,000 times more acute than ours, depending on the breed. What makes them so good at sniffing out scents? They possess up to 300 million olfactory receptors in their noses (compared to only about 6 million in humans). And the part of your dog's brain that controls smell is 40 times larger than ours. So yeah, that steak you're cooking really does smell good—even from three rooms away!

HE UNDERSTANDS MORE THAN YOU THINK

Dogs rely on our facial expressions and the tones of our voices to figure out if we're happy or angry. Using the canine version of "baby talk," i.e., speaking with exaggerated intonation, can also help your pup decipher what you want.

Dogs react more to the tone of a voice than the words being said.

HIS NOSE KNOWS

A dog's noseprint is as unique as a human fingerprint, and it can even be used for identification. In fact, the Canadian Kennel Club has been accepting noseprints as proof of identity since 1938!

The pores, lines and wrinkles on your dog's snout are unique.

PART 2

A DOG'S MIND

From that sensitive nose to her wagging tail and everything in between, here's how to decipher what your dog is really thinking.

HOW DOGS THINK

Ever wonder what's going through your
animal's mind as he shoots you a guilty look or comes
running when you call? Experts explain
that there's more going on than you would expect.

s any dog lover will tell you, dogs are highly intelligent animals. On average, they understand about 165 human words. They can sense our emotions; perceive dangers,from hidden weapons and illegal drugs to oncoming natural disasters; and even pick up on the presence of cancer or foretell an epileptic seizure before it happens.

So it may be tempting to assume that our canine companions feel and think just like humans do. But while many similarities between dogs and humans do exist—thanks, in part, to the 75 percent overlap in our genetic code—how dogs experience and understand reality is unique. Here's what science has been able to tell us so far about the canine mind, and why it's important to be mindful of their unique perspective.

DOG BRAIN 101

As with humans, the part of a dog's brain that enables sight (the occipital lobe) is located at the back of the skull, explains Stanley Coren, PhD, professor

The ratio of a dog's brain to his body is about 1:125. (A human brain is 1:50; a horse's, 1:600.)

emeritus in the department of psychology at the University of British Columbia and author of *The Wisdom of Dogs* (in addition to numerous other titles). The chunks that allow hearing (the temporal lobes) are located on the sides of a dog's brain. The motor cortex, which controls movement, is situated in a strip lining the top of the brain. The frontal lobes, which govern impulse control and cognitive feats like understanding that others have unique thoughts and feelings, are located behind a dog's forehead.

The size of these frontal lobes is one of the main differences between the human and dog brain, says Coren. That's why it can be harder for pups to reel in their impulses to bark, flee, bite or chew your favorite shoes to bits. Another significant difference is the size of the dog's olfactory bulb, a neural structure that enables smell and is 40 times larger in dogs than in humans. The size and complexity of this structure helps explain how—in combination with the design of a dog's nose and nasal cavities—dogs can sense our emotions, "sniff out" danger, differentiate friend from foe and make sense of their environment in ways that humans can only imagine.

INSIDE THEIR WORLD

Dogs essentially "see" through their noses. They smell through each nostril separately, which allows them to perceive the direction from which a smell is emanating, explains Alexandra Horowitz, an adjunct associate professor at Barnard College and the author of *Inside of a Dog*. They have separate pathways inside their nasal cavities: One for smelling, the other for inhaling. Dogs exhale through slits in the sides of their noses, which creates swirls of air that enhance odor concentrations to improve odor detection.

Horowitz, who also heads Barnard's Dog Cognition Lab, explains that a structure called the vomeronasal organ, which resides above a dog's mouth, specializes in picking up on hormones and other chemicals emitted by living things. These chemical signals communicate to dogs everything from a person's emotional state to what stage a woman is in her menstrual cycle, whether she is pregnant, whether someone has recently had sex (dogs tend to sniff the crotches of recently sexually active folks more intently) and whether someone is ill.

"A dog's nose can also pick up on the past and the future," says Horowitz. "Their scent receptors can detect the residue of other animals or objects that have passed through a given area, and they can anticipate a person's arrival by sensing that individual's signature aroma, wafting toward them from afar. In research, dogs

A dog's heightened senses explains why, for example, they react to an oncoming storm before we do.

With the exception of sight, a dog's senses are more highly developed than ours.

have also been shown to be highly reliable in picking out the smells of cancer." And anyone who has ever been to an airport or seen a crime show with a canine cameo already knows that dogs can be trained to detect bombs and illegal substances—even if such contraband is embedded in stinky socks or well-hidden inside luggage.

When it comes to sight, however, dogs are noticeably less equipped. "Dogs are very farsighted," says Coren, "meaning that objects close to their faces and bodies appear blurry." Smell helps compensate for

stability of the surface he's walking or running on," Coren says. The hypersensitivity of these nerve endings is why most dogs strongly dislike having their paws fondled.

Cuddlers should also take note that dogs are not really very fond of being hugged. "A dog experiences hugging as confining, restricting and anxiety-provoking," says Coren. But don't let this dissuade you from all physical contact with your pooch. A 2013 study found that petting and deep massage can slow the heart rate and lower levels of the stress hormone cortisol in stressed-out pups. As with

following another dog or human all indicate the need for attention and do not need to be learned," Coren explains. That also holds for dominance signals, like positioning a head over a rival dog's neck or back, staring down a rival, or mounting.

"Dogs indicate their perception of threat by snarling [with display of teeth], wagging the tip of an upright tail or fluffing out an upright tail," Coren adds. A high-held tail can also mean that your dog is in the mood to play—so long as it's paired with a "play bow," entailing elbows on the floor and hips held high.

If, however, a dog holds his tail between his legs, his ears are held flat against his head, his head is held low, or his eyes are averted from yours or another dog's, this is a sign of submission, says Coren. So too is lip-licking, freezing and then rolling onto her back.

The pitch of a dog's vocalizations indicates whether she is happy, sad, frightened, threatened, angry or upset. Coren explains that low-pitched growls typically indicate anger or imminent aggression. Low-pitched moans, however, can indicate pleasure and contentment. High-pitched whines indicate that a dog means no harm and is safe to approach. They can also be your dog's way of stating she is in pain—but in many cases can convey excitement, if paired with a wagging tail.

> ## Cancerous cells give off volatile organic compounds, which dogs are able to sniff out with their highly sensitive sense of smell.

this vision challenge, as does touch. "A dog's whiskers—also called vibrissae—serve as very sensitive touch receptors," Coren explains. "The sensation of air flowing through the vibrissae or the vibrissae's contact with another object or person communicates to a dog the shape and scope of objects in his vicinity—including whether a passage is too narrow to move through."

Dogs' paws also function as feedback hubs: "Highly sensitive nerve endings located in between the pads on the bottom of a dog's feet convey information about the

humans, "touch is crucial to forming emotional bonds," says Coren. This sense is also integral to dogs' ability to communicate with others, in the absence of language abilities.

HOW DOGS COMMUNICATE

Dogs don't have the linguistic ability to tell others, "Hey, quit it!" or "You're my best friend!" In lieu of verbal directives, they use a combination of touch, body language and vocalizations.

"Whining, wagging the tail with head held low, licking a person or fellow animal's face, pawing or

Dogs can speak volumes with their expressions.

Learn to read
your dog's emotions,
rather than assuming
they're just like ours.

CANINE EMOTIONS

Does all this mean that dogs experience a full range of emotions? The most definitive answer science has given us is: kind of. "Research indicates the average dog has a mind roughly equivalent to that of a human 2-and-a-half-year-old," says Coren. "That is to say that they have the basic emotions: fear, anger, happiness, surprise and disgust. But they have no complex social emotions like guilt, shame or pride."

So why might Rover look guilty when you come home to find he's soiled the rug again? Our perception of this emotional state may be more projection than understanding. "Your dog may be slinking around with his head down when you catch him after he's decorated your white carpet with her own earth tones," Coren says. "But he's most likely feeling fear, not guilt." That's because he's come to associate evidence of his indiscretion (unloading on your carpet) with bad things that happen to puppies who do this—or whatever form of punishment you respond with.

"Dogs aren't steeped in the same culture as we are," adds Horowitz. "Our attempts to convey 'Hey, chewing my shoes is wrong, and patiently waiting for me to come home is right' are very inconsistent and unlikely to be coherent to our dogs. When they show a 'guilty' look, they are most likely anticipating punishment, scolding or anger from a person who is very important to them—or they have learned an appeasement look to try to avoid that punishment or anger."

Horowitz cautions dog owners to reign in the assumption that dogs are just like us, only furrier and less smart. When we immediately anthropomorphize, she says, "we miss what might actually be happening with dogs that is not within human experience." What should you do? "Start from a position of not knowing [what your dog needs, wants or hopes for], then try to see what they tell you," Horowitz advises. "Dogs are constantly communicating to and with us, and it behooves us to pay attention to what they are saying, what they need and what they understand about our shared world." 🐾

> Dogs don't experience complex emotions like guilt—that look she gives you after making a mess is fear.

Do Dogs Experience Empathy?

IT'S REASSURING TO THINK that if you are somehow hurt, your dog will come to comfort you because she feels your pain. And research has shown that if a person is showing distress (such as crying), a dog is more likely to go over and try to make physical contact with him or her.

"This willingness to stay close to and comfort people who are distressed or showing signs of discomfort is how researchers measure empathy in children," says researcher Stanley Coren, adding that this quality also makes canines quite useful in pet therapy.

Dogs' ability to pick up on our emotions may lie more in their perception of the chemical signals we give off when we're experiencing happiness, sadness, anger or fear than in their replication of our emotional experiences inside their minds, research suggests. So it isn't clear whether they can actually "feel" the exact way we're feeling—a crucial component of human empathy, some argue. But if an inclination to help another who's suffering is a hallmark of this capacity, then dogs may indeed possess empathy, no matter how the experience manifests in their brains.

LEARNING THE LANGUAGE OF DOGS

Dogs have developed a vocal language, including barking, just to communicate with humans—so maybe it's time we learned how to "speak dog."

ountless videos uploaded to social media reveal the same scenario: dogs barking and their humans asking, "what?"—as if the dogs are suddenly going to start speaking English. While that's not about to happen, it is possible to glean what dogs are trying to say by understanding their various vocalizations and the variables within those sounds.

Dogs communicate with the world around them, and with humans, by using a number of different sounds—including barking, baying or howling, whining, growling, yelping, groaning and sighing—as well as with their body language. While some of these sounds are obvious, like a yelp when you accidently step on a dog's tail, the bark is the most difficult to decipher because its meaning and sound quality changes: a dog barking when the doorbell rings sounds different than the bark of a dog that's excited to go for a walk.

Humans have had a lot of time to understand

the language of dogs because they were domesticated tens of thousands of years ago and have worked by our sides ever since. However, recent research has revealed a far more nuanced understanding of what dogs are really trying to tell us when they bark or sigh or growl.

"Dogs are genetically modified organisms, meaning that over time humans have bred dogs whose behaviors they found useful to make more dogs that are likely to exhibit those desirable behaviors," says Lauren Novack, a canine behaviorist at Behavior Vets of NYC. "Now that we're keeping working dogs as companion animals, those behaviors—like alert barking or howling—are still elicited by the environment, but are not always welcome."

For example, beagles bay because they were selectively bred to hunt small animals by surrounding the animal and literally keeping it "at bay" until the human hunter arrived at the scene. The hunter would be drawn to the location by following the very loud baying sound, which is capable of carrying over long distances when the dogs are out of sight.

Of course, if you have a beagle as a pet, that same baying can be a problem, especially if you live in close proximity to your neighbor. Just remember, before a dog owner can work with a dog on issues like barking or baying, it's important to figure out why the dog is barking and what she is trying to say.

WHAT BARKS MEAN

To understand what a dog is trying to communicate by barking, we have to pay attention to the bark's "three dimensions," says Stanley Coren, professor emeritus in the department of psychology at the University of British Columbia and well-known expert on the language of dogs. These three dimensions are pitch, duration and the frequency, or repetition rate, of the sounds.

A low-pitched bark indicates the perception of a threat, anger, or aggression, and a high-pitched bark means the opposite, says Coren, indicating that it's safe to approach.

Some interpretations, of course, depend on breed. For example, the bark of a German shepherd is naturally more alarming than the bark of a Yorkshire terrier. In terms of meaning, pitch is relevant, but nonetheless varies according to the individual dog.

The situation the dog finds himself in has meaning, too, and context is critical. For instance, Kathryn Lord of the University of Massachusetts and Mark Feinstein of Hampshire College report that dogs have adapted their bark to better communicate with their human companions.

A team of researchers from Budapest, Hungary, has drilled down more, finding true nuance in

Play-fighting between dogs is great exercise, but watch carefully so it doesn't turn real.

Animal behaviorists look to pioneering studies conducted over the past decade to penetrate the vocalizations of dogs.

the meaning of the bark. That group has found that shorter barks sound more positive, and high-pitched noises more intense and negative, to the human ear. Humans, the researchers note, use these same variations in pitch to read the emotional state of other humans.

The Hungarian scientists also report that meaning varies according to the "three dimensions" of duration, pitch and repetition described by Coren. A pooch who wants a treat barks differently along these dimensions than one feeling anxious or scared.

To pinpoint meaning more specifically, animal behaviorist and veterinarian Sophia Yin recorded the barking of 10 different dogs across three situations: disturbance (a doorbell ringing); isolation (a dog locked outside away from its owner); and play.

She discovered that low-pitched barks with a harsh tone and little variation in pitch or loudness indicated a "disturbance," like a stranger at the door. These barks are at full volume and sometimes so frequent that they appear to fuse into what Yin refers to as "superbarks."

High-pitched barking with more tonal and frequency changes may indicate what Yin calls an "isolation bark"—when the dog is

A snarling face can indicate that a dog is under a bit of stress.

left alone, for example. This type of bark often occurs as one single bark at a time (a little like yelling, "Hey!"). A play bark is similar in pitch to the isolation bark, but play barks occur in clusters.

IF YOUR DOG COULD SPEAK ENGLISH

If you really want to understand your dog, you have to observe the whole picture. That includes a dog's body language as well as the ABCs of behavior analysis, says Kayla Fratt, a canine behaviorist at Journey Dog Training in Missoula, Montana.

The ABCs is an acronym for "antecedent, behavior, and consequence," a sequence of steps

for translating barks. In the first step, examine behavior and body language right before the bark. In the second step, examine the bark itself: Was the dog showing his teeth or practicing a bow? Finally, what happened right after the bark? Did your pooch receive water, attention, a favorite toy?

If two dogs are playing, Fratt says, and one or both dogs bark but nonetheless continue to play with relaxed and happy body language, we can assume that it was a play bark. "But it's a very different type of bark if the antecedent is that the dogs are playing, and then the dog barks, and then he nips at his playmate, and then the play stops or escalates into a fight."

By observing your dog's body language in both situations, you will be able to read the signs and act before any negative consequences occur.

The same technique can be applied to other vocalizations that dogs produce. If you're walking your dog, and a stranger approaches you aggressively demanding your wallet, the sound of your dog's low-pitched growling is a definite warning. If the warning is not heeded, growling may turn into aggressive behavior.

But some dogs growl when they want you to play with them. In this case, you will notice relaxed body language, such as the ears in their normal position or slightly forward and the tail raised and wagging. You might also notice the "play-bow" position, with the front legs extended like the dog is about to lie down with his butt in the air.

Another vocalization dogs use to communicate is whining, a high-pitched sound made with the mouth closed. Like a whining toddler, the dog usually wants something, such as a toy stuck under the couch, food or to go outside. But a whine can also indicate frustration, anxiety, stress or simply that the dog wants attention.

"It's dependent on the individual dog," says Fratt. Does the dog want a treat? Does he want to play? Does he want to go outside? "Usually, if you start trying to think of it in that context, you can figure out what they're looking for." Just beware that (like a toddler) if your dog whines when he wants a treat, you are reinforcing the behavior if you give him one each time.

Dogs issue rich combinations of sounds—groans, sighs, yelps, howls and whimpers—and the meanings are multiple and complex. For instance, yelping usually indicates pain, though a dog that yelps may just be surprised. (See the sidebar, right, for a more detailed explanation.) Today, thanks to tremendous strides in the study of canine cognition, it's easier to understand your dog. You just have

The Six Basic Sounds of Dog Language

THE AMERICAN KENNEL CLUB RECOGNIZES SIX BASIC COMPONENTS OF DOG LANGUAGE:

1 BARKING
While some dogs just naturally bark more than others, a bark can mean different things. Pay attention to the situation and the pitch, duration and frequency of the barking.

2 WHINING
A dog whines mostly when he wants something. It's their version of "Mom, Mom, Mom!"

3 GROWLING
A growl is usually a warning to back off, but sometimes dogs growl when they play. Look at the body language to discern the difference.

4 SIGHING
A dog that sighs is contented— or deeply disappointed in you!

5 HOWLING AND BAYING
Howling is usually a response to a high-pitched sound, like a siren. Wolves howl to communicate with their pack. Breeds like beagles and hounds, meanwhile, are bred to emit prolonged bays to alert hunters during a chase.

6 GROANING
A dog may groan because of muscle or joint pain. There's a condition called ascites (fluid in the abdomen) that makes dogs groan when lying down.

This smiling mixed pit bull terrier is most surely looking right at his favorite human.

> Dogs definitely smile. A wide grin on your pooch generally means he's feeling good.

Reading Body Language

IF YOU DON'T learn how to read a dog's body language, it will be much harder to interpret his vocalizations. Here are seven major areas of body language to help your dog communicate with the world:

● **EYES**
A dog with a lot of white showing in the eyes, called "whale eyes," is stressed or afraid. A squinting dog is at peace.

● **EARS**
Ears in their natural position indicates a relaxed dog. Ears back and flattened to the skull—not so much.

● **MOUTH**
Yes, dogs smile, and it means they're happy. But a dog with a tense jaw and lips pulled back is stressed. Curled lips and bared teeth signal aggression.

● **HAIR**
The expression "made my hair stand on end" applies to dogs too, but it's called raised hackles, and it indicates aggression, fear or excitement.

● **SWEATING OR PANTING**
If the dog is breathing with short, fast breaths (panting) and a tight mouth, this could indicate anxiety. Dog sweat glands are located in the paws; a dog sweating so heavily he leaves wet footprints could be distressed.

● **TAIL**
You can tell a lot from a dog's tail, but wagging doesn't always mean the dog is happy. A tail raised and wagging back and forth rapidly, called "flagging," indicates a dog about to defend itself by attacking. A rigid tail held high means the dog is aroused.

● **BODY POSTURE**
A dog who is crouched low to the ground is afraid. But when the front end of the dog is lower than the rear, that generally indicates a fearful, aggressive dog.

Signs of a happy dog? A mouth slightly open, with a relaxed tongue and facial expression.

Dogs can tell us a lot about their emotions without having to say a single word!

WHAT YOUR DOG IS REALLY SAYING

Learn how to read the common—and sometimes surprising—signals that dogs are trying to send us.

Y ou probably think you know what your dog is trying to say. His tail wags—he's happy. He rolls over— belly rub! And of course, that whine in the kitchen is a surefire cue that he simply wants his supper.

But your dog is also probably sending you other, more subtle signals that you are simply not getting. "It's just like human body language, where you pick up cues like hand-wringing, lip-licking and yawning," says dog trainer Kris Denny, owner of Petlandia Pet Care in Portland, Oregon. "Dogs are the same way: They're constantly sending us messages, but the average person doesn't always pick up on them." The easiest way to suss out a dog's body language is to assess his TEMP—short for tail, eyes, mouth and posture, says Laurie Coger, DVM, owner of the Healthy Dog Workshop in Albany, New York. "Those four areas will tell you a lot about what a dog is thinking." Ready to decipher all that your dog is trying to communicate? Check out the following things she may be saying with her body language.

TAIL

We tend to put tail-wagging into two major categories. A wagging tail means your dog is happy and excited; if it's tucked between his legs, he may be feeling a little timid. But the tail can also be a signal of so much more, says Coger.

Dogs are more likely to yawn or lick their lips when they're nervous.

- **Straight Up** "When a dog sticks his tail straight in the air, he's trying to make himself look bigger so he doesn't have to fight," notes Coger.
- **Horizontal** A tail straight out indicates that he/she is sizing up the situation; the dog is alert but not necessarily taking an aggressive stance.
- **The Low, Slow Wag** This is an indication that your dog is feeling nervous and may be getting ready to pounce. "It's similar to something you might see with a cat," says Coger.
- **Left or Right** A 2013 Italian study found that the direction of a tail wag matters: Wagging more to the right can be a sign of companionship and friendliness, while a left-leaning wag can indicate anxiety.

EYES

Eyes are the windows to the soul—but if you pay attention, they can also cue you in on a dog's mood.

- **Hard Eye Contact** While eye contact is generally thought to be a good thing, particularly among humans, that's not always the case with canines. "Dogs making eye contact can mean anything from 'Is it time for a treat?' to assessing whether you're a threat," says Coger. "That's why it's always important to talk to the owner to interpret the meaning of the stare-down. With some dogs, when they are assessing you at first, it's best to ignore them until they have decided you're not a threat."
- **Soft Eye Contact** Unlike hard eye contact, which can be a dog's way to decide if you're safe, soft eye contact is a way of showing love. Think of this as a more relaxed look, often half squinting, with an adoring gaze rather than a stare. "Once trust is very well-established with a dog, soft and extended eye contact can be bonding during a snuggle or while relaxing and is typically reserved for family members or very trusted friends," says Denny. She adds that this eye contact helps release the "love" hormone, oxytocin, in your dog's brain.
- **Showing the Whites** Seeing the whites of a dog's eyes—called oil or whale eye—is a common stress signal. "It's a displacement behavior, where the dog is trying to look away from and escape the situation," explains Denny. "It's one of the first cues we see when a dog is slightly uncomfortable."

MOUTH

"Religion is a smile on a dog," sings Edie Brickell in "What I Am." But not all dog smiles are alike, says Coger.

- **Pulling Teeth Back** This is what's known as a submissive grin, where a dog pulls his teeth back slightly to show he's not a threat either to other animals or people (sometimes you'll see it on those guilty-dog photos going around Facebook).

● **Licking Lips and Panting** These are generally nervous gestures that can signal stress or discomfort.

● **Yawning** Just like people, dogs yawn—but not just because they are tired. Yawning can sometimes be a sign that a dog is stressed and wants to leave the situation, explains Coger. On the other hand, yawning can also signal excitement (like when your dog is waiting to go on her walk and, in her opinion, you're taking too long).

POSTURE

Dogs can say a lot through a stance.

● **Hackling/Stiffening** While hackling (raising the hairs that run along a dog's back from neck to tail) is typically a dog's attempt to look bigger, it depends on the context. "Hackling is one of the many signals we can observe in a dog when they are aroused or stimulated by something in their environment," says Denny. "If you see it along with freezing and showing the whites of their eyes, the dog may be about to snap. But if it's the only sign, it could indicate excitement."

● **Leaning Away** Just like humans may try to get away from something that's bothering us, dogs can do the same with their body language, adds Denny. "If a dog is looking away or ignoring the situation, that dog is saying he's not comfortable."

● **Shaking Off** Beyond getting rid of water, a dog shaking his body can be a sign of anxiety, says Denny. "The dog is literally shaking off the stressful situation," she explains. ❖

Your dog may lick your face to show affection, or to get some attention.

DOG BEHAVIOR, EXPLAINED

The scoop on why they sniff, pee, lick, roll and more.

Ever wonder why your dog does so many quirky things that you'll only see among canines? "Dogs still hang on to some of the holdover behaviors from when they were not domesticated, but they've figured out how to successfully live with humans for thousands of years, which has also affected how they act," notes Sarah Fraser, co-founder of Instinct Dog Behavior and Training in New York and a certified dog-behavior consultant. Take a look at some popular theories behind these unique canine behaviors.

Why Do Dogs...
ROLL IN NASTY STUFF?

It's inevitable—we'll be out for a walk in the park off-leash, and my 5-year-old Lab mix, Trixie, will find the stinkiest, smelliest something-or-other to roll in.

12–14 hours
Amount of time most dogs typically sleep in a day

Despite my pleas and scolding, it's a behavior that persists whenever she's given the opportunity…and an utter (frustrating!) mystery to me.

But Fraser explains that certain dogs are attracted to nasty smells like decomposing animals as a holdover from when they were hunter-scavengers. "It helps to mask their scent from prey," she says. Then again, it could just be the, umm, interesting smell. "Just like some humans like perfume or jewelry, some dogs think this strong scent is interesting and even attractive—after all, dogs are very olfactory."

Why Do Dogs…
TURN IN A CIRCLE BEFORE LYING DOWN?
Some dogs do this multiple times; others, just once. Animal behaviorists theorize this could be some evolutionary holdover, checking around for threats before bedding down for the night. Others note it may be an instinct to chase away possible vermin or search for uncomfortable stones or twigs that can poke them as they sleep. But psychologist and dog researcher Stanley Coren, PhD, says it may be more a matter of creating a comfy spot to snooze in. He studied 62 dogs and found that only 19 percent turned at least one full circle before lying down on a smooth surface. But on a shag carpet with an uneven surface, more than half the dogs (55 percent) turned at least once before settling in. "This data indicates that one reason dogs are spinning

about is to make themselves a more comfortable temporary 'nest' to nap in," he writes in *Psychology Today*.

Why Do Dogs…
TWITCH THEIR LEGS WHEN THEY SLEEP?
Chasing rabbits or a squirrel in a midday nap sounds like a pretty good way for most dogs to spend their afternoon. And dogs *do* dream, according to research studies—which have found that dogs have the same type of slow-wave sleep and rapid eye movement (REM) patterns we do. It's during the REM stage that dogs (and people) dream—as indicated by those rolling eyes, twitching paws and sharp yelps as they slumber. Note that both younger and older dogs seem to dream more than middle-aged pooches.

Why Do Dogs…
MARK THEIR TERRITORY?
You probably sign your name at the end of an email or letter to identify yourself. That's not too different from how a dog communicates to others. When a dog pees on a spot, he's staking his claim to the area. Unneutered dogs are generally more assertive and more prone to marking than neutered ones. "It's all an exchange," says Fraser. "Dogs can learn a lot of information about things, like another dog's gender, age and even potential reproductive status, just by sniffing where that dog has peed." And when a dog lifts his leg in the house, it's often a sign

of anxiety or a need to claim his place when there's a new animal (or person) in the house.

Why Do Dogs…
SNIFF EACH OTHER'S BUTTS WHEN THEY FIRST MEET?
One can only imagine humans greeting each other by offering up their backsides—yet among dogs, it's the preferred method of salutation. That's because dogs have a notably better sense of smell, and the anal sacs located near their butts contain glands secreting chemicals that provide lots of interesting information about things such as gender, reproductive status and even the dog's emotional state, including how friendly or aggressive he is. "It goes way beyond what the dog ate for dinner," explains Fraser. And because dogs have a good memory for scents, they can also identify dogs they haven't seen for years, since each dog (like each person) has their own unique smell.

Why Do Dogs…
LICK OUR FACES?
Puppies lick out of instinct—it's their way of gathering information about the world around them. "It's also a way of a dog communicating: 'I am not a threat,'" explains Fraser. And when your dog covers your face with kisses as you walk through the front door? She's probably just overjoyed to see you—and wants to let you know.
— *Alyssa Shaffer* 🐾

The body language of these dogs shows how much they love attention from their human.

PART 3

HELPING EACH OTHER

Your dog can do amazing things—you may just have
to give her a little extra TLC to get there.

LISTEN UP

Getting your dog to do what you want involves love, patience—and a whole lot of treats. A top vet shares her best advice for training that gets results.

A generation ago, training your pet was all about establishing who was top dog. "We used to think it was important to show a dog who was boss and to establish dominance, so they would do what you said just because you told them to," notes Jennifer Summerfield, DVM, a veterinarian and professional dog trainer based in Wayne, West Virginia, and the author of *Train Your Dog Now!*

Today, most dog trainers agree that positivity is the way to go when it comes to having your pooch behave. "We've discovered, from working with other species, that you don't need to punish a dog to make him behave. In fact, that can produce a lot of stress and anxiety or aggressive behavior," says Summerfield. Animals, in general, learn best by using positive reinforcement, she notes. "You are much better off focusing on what the dog is doing right and rewarding him for that behavior."

THE POWER OF POSITIVITY

This type of positive reinforcement will result in the behaviors you want, adds Summerfield. Getting her to sit, stay, come and walk well on a leash are all integral parts of that. But it also works in reverse. If your dog is doing something you don't like—jumping on company, gnawing on your loafers—don't punish her. Instead, says Summerfield, make sure good behavior

is reinforced and that bad behavior won't lead to anything your dog likes. "Focus on whether you can teach the dog to do something different by redirecting her to do something else and rewarding that behavior." It's a lot quicker and more straightforward for the dog to understand, she adds. "They get: 'Do this and you'll get a reward' rather than: 'Don't do that.'"

The easiest form of positive reinforcement? Offer a treat. This can be ordinary kibble or dog biscuits, although you may need to bring out what Summerfield calls "the big guns"—fancier and more flavorful fare like hot dog slices, string cheese, shredded chicken or freeze-dried liver bits. Use these treats in a precise way, providing a reward at the exact moment your dog does what you ask. It also helps to build a positive environment for your dog, so she is more likely to listen to you during training. "Adjust the value of the reward to the difficulty of the task and the environment," she adds.

In addition, keep your training sessions short, especially at the beginning. "Often, owners will push their dogs too far, or expect them to do too much, too soon," says Summerfield. "The key is taking baby steps." So if your dog is sitting perfectly in the comfort of your living room, don't necessarily expect that he will do the same task in the middle of the park. "For the most part, dogs don't generalize well and need to practice a lot before they have mastered a skill."

Remember too that yelling at your dog *after* he's stolen the roast off the table or peed on the rug won't be helpful. "If something has already happened, it's no longer a training opportunity," says Summerfield. "There is nothing you can do with the situation that will have an impact so he won't do it again." Rather, she says, think about why that situation occurred and what you can do about it in the future. That involves being proactive: Don't leave food on the counter where your dog can reach it; take your dog out regularly to cut down on the risk of accidents.

Finally, keep in mind that while we tend to think of puppies as the ones who need all the training, dogs at any age can be taught to change their behavior. "That line of not being able to teach an old dog new tricks is just a myth," says Summerfield. "Dogs can always adapt their behavior and learn and grow." 🐾

A 3-month-old puppy can usually "hold it" for up to four hours—so don't punish him if he messes up.

> **The best way to encourage good behavior is to give a yummy reward right after your dog does what you ask.**

Give your dog plenty of exercise and mental stimulation, and he will be better behaved.

CANINE CARE

10 THINGS YOUR VET WISHES YOU WOULD DO

Here's advice from top veterinarians on
how to make sure your pooch stays healthy and happy.

When you bring your dog home for the first time, she's likely a (fur) ball full of energy—healthy, happy, with tons of spunk. But over time, she might start to develop aches, pains, itches and other issues that can affect her well-being and quality of life. That's why it's important to follow your veterinarian's advice as closely as possible."Your vet is your friend—you'll want to talk to him or her about any issues your pet has before taking advice from Dr. Google or your local pet-store worker," says Millie Rosales, DVM, founder of Miami Veterinary Dermatology. Here, some dog docs share their best tips for keeping your pet lively and fit, with more wag in her tail.

The average dog-owning household makes a visit to the vet 2.6 times a year.

VET WISH NO. 1
Take your dog's dental health seriously.

It may seem like a nuisance to brush your dog's teeth daily (or at least two or three times per week) and bring him in for annual dental cleanings. But letting your dog's oral health slide can be harmful. "People should understand just how much it hurts to have severe dental disease," says Jessica Vogelsang, DVM, a San Diego–based veterinarian and author of *All Dogs Go to Kevin*. "A lot of times, when people tell us their elderly dog is 'slowing down,' the dog is actually suffering from a mouth of rotting teeth," she notes. "And once it's fixed, they're like puppies again." Although it may sound easier to get an anesthesia-free cleaning at your local pet store, those cleanings are purely cosmetic—unlike during a vet's cleaning, they don't get under the gums, where the disease really lives.

VET WISH NO. 2
Stop trying to solve allergy issues on your own.

If your dog starts developing an itch, you may want to begin experimenting with things like his food—but fight the urge. "I often see dogs placed on a grain-free diet recommended by a pet-store clerk, but it's a big misconception that grain-free diets help skin problems," shares Rosales.

Instead, book an appointment with your veterinarian when signs like nonstop scratching, chewing or licking first appear. Your vet will soon figure out what's up and will be able to suggest the best treatment for the problem, such as allergy vaccines. Just know that it's important to take your dog in sooner rather than later. "I often find that if we diagnose a dog with environmental allergies early on, they respond better to immunotherapy than pets that have had the condition for years," adds Rosales.

VET WISH NO. 3
Don't let your dog find snacks outside.

Chances are, your four-legged friend likes to sniff—and sometimes eat—whatever is in his path. But when it comes to food on the ground, be it stuff that's growing or discarded grub, make sure to divert his attention before he goes in for a bite. Consider wild mushrooms. "Only experts can tell poisonous mushrooms from safe ones, so avoiding all wild mushrooms is the safest thing to do," says David Dorman, DVM, PhD, a professor of toxicology at the College of Veterinary Medicine at North Carolina State University. "Eating just a few bites of certain poisonous mushrooms can cause liver damage that can kill your pet," he adds. Trashed items, like a scrap of sandwich or bit of cheese, may also harm your pooch if they've been contaminated. Steer your dog away, even if the food looks relatively harmless to you.

Annual checkups are important for your dog (and you), so you can catch any signs of trouble early on.

VET WISH NO. 4
Keep heartworm meds up to date.

"Heartworm disease is on the rise across the country, due to both warmer temperatures and dogs traveling around more freely," says Vogelsang. At the same time, the percentage of dogs getting heartworm-prevention medication is on the decline, according to a study in the journal *Parasites & Vectors*. "People think, because it takes six months for a larvae to mature into an adult, that they can give the heartworm pill once every few months and it'll be fine—but that's not how it works," she says. The American Heartworm Society recommends following the Think 12 rule: Give your dog 12 months of heartworm prevention and have them tested for heartworm every 12 months. And just because your dog is on preventative medication doesn't mean he's in the clear—a missed or late dose could still put him at risk for infection, which is why that yearly check is necessary.

VET WISH NO. 5
Seek help for ear infections pronto.

When your dog starts whimpering and pawing at his ears, you may chalk it up to his latest bath or a swim at the lake, but it could be another problem. "Some owners think that water in their ears causes infections, but this isn't always the case—many ear infections happen because of allergies," says Rosales.

That's especially true for dogs already prone to skin allergies; plus ear mites and hyperthyroidism may also cause infections. So instead of trying out natural-remedy cures at home, book an appointment with your veterinarian right away. Your dog will likely need medication and a professional ear cleaning, and the faster he gets it, the easier it will be to deal with the problem, adds Rosales. Remember that major health issues, such as hearing loss or facial paralysis, can happen if ear infections aren't treated.

VET WISH NO. 6
Focus on food quality, not marketing.

"Nutrition is one of the most controversial parts of pet ownership out there, thanks to savvy marketers and 'experts,'" says Vogelsang. Many owners are choosing grain-free foods for their dogs, made by new and boutique companies that don't do enough quality-assurance testing. "Grains aren't the enemy; in fact, dogs have evolved enzymes in their saliva to dissolve starch," she notes. The Food and Drug Administration recently announced a possible connection between an increase in canine heart disease and diets high in ingredients, such as legumes and potatoes, that are common in grain-free food. A veterinary nutritionist can help you pick the best food, based on your dog's age and health. Looking to avoid store-bought stuff altogether? "The vast majority of recipes online are not balanced, though you can absolutely do it right, with a veterinary nutritionist's help," adds Vogelsang.

Just like people, dogs need a healthy balance of protein, carbs and fats in each of their meals.

Always keep
a close eye
on your dog
when he's
outdoors. Pups
are naturally
curious!

Be careful
where he sniffs:
Dogs can pick up
life-threatening
fungal infections
in damp soil.

VET WISH NO. 7
Don't just let your dog out in the backyard.

It's nice that your dog has outdoor space. But when he goes to get some fresh air, Sparky likely heads to his favorite spot and rests there until it's time to come back in. "Many dogs need interaction with another dog or their owners in order to get an appropriate amount of exercise while in the yard," says Susan Nelson, DVM, clinical professor at Kansas State University College of Veterinary Medicine.

Schedule more active minutes with your pooch. The goal: between 30 minutes and two hours of daily exercise, depending on the type of dog. Small breeds (and older dogs of all breeds) may need only a stroll around the neighborhood, while dogs in the hunting, working and herding groups, like Australian shepherds and border collies, require much more. "If your dog doesn't receive enough daily activity, they may turn to destructive behaviors and could suffer from obesity-related health issues," says Hyunmin Kim, DVM, veterinary staff manager at ASPCA Community Medicine. And dog obesity is a serious problem in this country—more than 56 percent of dogs are obese or overweight, and the number continues to rise each year, according to the Association for Pet Obesity Prevention. Walks and fetch are a great start, but you can also set up agility games in your yard, go to your local dog park (just make sure he's had all his shots) or invite other pooches over for playdates. Your dog will also get extra socialization—a win-win!

VET WISH NO. 8
Poison-proof your home.

"Most pet-poisoning cases happen at home," warns Dorman. Go through your house room by room and lock up any chemicals, cleaners or other potentially poisonous substances, like laundry pods and weed killers. (For a full list of what's hazardous, visit aspca.org/pet-care/animal-poison-control.) "Dogs will try to eat anything—and they don't know the difference between the things that can harm them and those that can help them," says Dorman. Even if a product doesn't look remotely edible to you (hello, fertilizer!) your dog might still find it worthy of at least a few nibbles. And keep in mind, certain foods can be toxic to your pooch, including onions, garlic, chocolate, grapes, macadamia nuts, salt and the sweetener xylitol. Keep these items off the counter and out of reach.

VET WISH NO. 9
Trust dog vaccines and keep them up to date.

You may have seen headlines saying that some dog owners are forgoing vaccinations for their pups because of worries that the injections could potentially cause autism or other concerns. But there's no reliable scientific evidence that supports

this, says the British Veterinary Association, which came out with a statement to debunk this myth, which is also pervasive among some parents. As with people, vaccines are crucial for preventing illness in dogs, and they up the odds that your pet will live a long, healthy life, according to the ASPCA. "People often underrate the severity of many of the diseases we vaccinate against, especially in puppies—Parvo is brutal, and rabies can kill not only your dog but also you," says Vogelsang. Talk with your veterinarian about which vaccines your dog needs and the right timeline, depending on his age and medical history. Lifestyle also plays a role—for example, if your dog boards in a kennel, slurps lake water or lives around livestock: These factors mean that your dog may require additional shots to stay healthy.

VET WISH NO. 10
Discuss supplements with a professional.

Notice your dog is a little less mobile than he used to be? It might be time to talk to your veterinarian about supplements. "Dogs, just like humans, can benefit from joint supplements and omega-3 fatty acids as they get older," says Kim. Vets often suggest glucosamine to help ease pain that can come along with

arthritis, and omega-3s to help reduce inflammation in the joints. Just don't assume that human supplements are good for dogs— they might include additional ingredients that are safe only for people. Plus, human vitamins (like vitamin D and iron) and herbal supplements can actually poison your dog, according to the ASPCA. Bottom line: Give your dog only the type of supplement and dose that's recommended by your vet. 🐾

If your dog spends a lot of time outdoors, he may require additional vaccinations.

Your dog produces 13 of the 23 amino acids that make up the building blocks of protein; the rest must come from his diet.

COPING WITH ANXIETIES

If your pet panics at being left alone or gets the shakes during a thunderstorm, here's what can calm her down—and keep her from freaking out in the first place.

W hen we first adopted our greyhound, Holly, from a race track in Hollywood, Florida, we expected her to have a few quirks as she settled into her new life in New York City. Surprisingly, though, loud noises like sirens and car horns didn't really seem to bother her. What did cause her to turn tail and start shaking? The Goodyear blimp. Turns out that whenever our sight hound spotted an unidentified flying object (kites, balloons and low-flying planes also did the trick), like the blimp—which often cruised up and down the Hudson River on weekends—she'd go into extreme anxiety mode. There was almost nothing we could do,

short of getting her back inside ASAP, to help her calm down.

While not many other dogs I've known have shared this particular anxiety, over the course of our adopting several greyhounds and one spunky Lab mix, our dogs have all had one thing or another that spooked them. Paris hid in the bathtub whenever there was thunder. Jett gnawed the bars of his crate when we left him alone. Trixie barks like crazy when food delivery shows up at our door.

So why do some dogs have certain triggers, and what can we do to help them settle down and feel happier? "As a rule, dogs have a lot fewer psychological hang-ups than

Cannabis-derived oils
or tablets can be used
to calm your pet without
getting him high.

Anxiety can lead to chewing (shoes are a popular target).

people do," notes Gary Richter, DVM, medical director of Holistic Veterinary Care in Oakland, California, and a veterinary health expert with rover.com. "But like people, dogs can develop certain anxieties that can manifest in a variety of ways." And while some dogs may be naturally more nervous than others, early development and the animal's environment can also play a role in any fears or anxieties. "It can be a genetic issue, but life experience also counts," adds Richter.

If your dog has developed an anxiety that doesn't seem to be getting better and is causing discomfort, it may be time to bring in the experts. In more extreme cases, both your vet and a behavioral expert may be needed to figure out a plan that works, says Terran Tull, a certified dog trainer and behavior consultant for Best Friends Animal Society. "If you notice any change in behavior, it's important to start with your vet to rule out any health concern," says Tull. The next step is to figure out what is triggering the anxiety and then address it. Luckily, there are a number of ways you can help your dog feel better.

START EARLY

The sooner you can look at the problem, the better —especially if you're dealing with a puppy. Studies have shown that puppies who are desensitized to noises like fireworks, thunder and other loud noises are less likely to develop noise phobias when they are older. "There is a period from as young as 3 weeks through about 12 to 20 weeks that is a critical socialization period for puppies," says Tull. If dogs aren't properly socialized in this time frame, they can carry a number of anxieties forward as they grow up. If possible, introduce your dog to a wide variety of people, sounds and new places when they are young, she says. (Note that until your pup has received all her immunizations, you'll still need to keep her away from well-trafficked places, like dog runs and indoor play spaces.) "Little by little, try to expose your dog to as many positive experiences as you can," adds Tull. "Each time, offer treats, toys and praise to make her feel comfortable."

Already adopted or living with a dog that's past her early puppyhood? No worries, says Tull. Make sure your dog has had time to settle into her new digs, then gradually introduce her around the neighborhood and to family and friends. "Dogs make all their decisions on how they feel in the moment—if they think they are safe, they will be a lot more comfortable and relaxed," adds Tull.

CONSIDER MEDICATIONS

Conventional medications may have their place, but several drug-free remedies can also

14%
Number
of dogs that
suffer from
separation
anxiety

As hard as it may be, don't encourage your dog's fears by picking her up or petting her when she shows signs that she's afraid. It's best to remain calm so she knows everything's OK.

Keep some background noise—like a radio or the TV—going when you leave, as company.

help to calm an anxious canine, although they should still be used in conjunction with behavioral modifications. "Several types of herbal therapies can help to assuage anxiety long enough for a dog to calm down and accept training," says Richter.

Herbs such as valerian and kava kava, and traditional Chinese medicinal herbs, can all have a calming effect in dogs, as can certain forms of medical cannabis, like CBD. The latter is growing widely in popularity as medical marijuana continues to become legalized throughout the U.S. and Canada. Unlike marijuana, however, CBD contains none of the psychoactive ingredient THC (the active substance that causes marijuana's high), so it's safe for dogs. Some dog owners also like the combo of treatments found in Rescue Remedy, a mix of natural herb and flower extracts that has been known to help calm dogs down (look for the pet-specific blend).

If your pooch still isn't responding properly, talk to your vet about pharmaceutical remedies that may provide some stronger measure of relief. SSRIs and antidepressants (similar to the medications given to humans for anxiety) are occasionally prescribed for dogs coping with anxiety; medications such as benzodiazepine plus an antidepressant may be used on an occasion when you know your dog will be anxious (for

example, on July 4, for a dog who is fearful of fireworks.) Never give your dog a medication (herbal or pharmaceutical) meant for a human: While the ingredients may be similar, the dosing is not—and you can easily overdose your dog or cause some unwanted drug interactions.

EASE IN

In addition to medications, experts often recommend a desensitization process for dogs with anxieties. The process allows you to gradually expose your pooch to whatever might be bothering her. "With desensitization, you are deliberately exposing the dog, in small amounts, to whatever might be causing some trauma," says Tull. For example, if your dog is frightened by thunder, you can search for a recording on YouTube and then play it on your computer or phone at a very low volume. Gradually make the volume louder and louder until your dog no longer is bothered by the noise.

Desensitization is typically accompanied by another behavioral training called counterconditioning, which works

to change your dog's response to whatever is causing him to be anxious from negative to positive. Offer an extra-special treat every time the dog is exposed to the perceived threat. That translates to the scary thing (thunder) bringing a positive reward (shredded chicken breast!). "Over time, your dog will start to recognize the threat simply as a chance to get a treat," says Tull. Try to give the treat as soon as possible after being exposed to the perceived threat so your dog can connect something good happening with the thing he once thought was really scary.

Most of all, be patient. Just like with people, most dog anxieties don't go away in just a couple of positive interactions. "It's important to keep up the training or whatever else you are using to help the dog stay comfortable—there's almost always a little underlying current that may be causing dismay, and that has to be worked through," says Tull. "Dogs can't really say what's bothering them, and some just take longer to adjust. It's a continued process—but eventually you will get there."
—*Alyssa Shaffer* 🐾

> Animal behaviorists say exposure therapy—a little at a time—can help desensitize an anxious dog to the events that frighten her.

Ask your vet about medicines or herbs that may help relieve your dog's anxieties.

ADOPTION

RESCUE ME

Millions of dogs sit in shelters, waiting for a chance at finding their forever home. Here's how you can save the day—and change your own life.

By the time this book comes out, I will likely have adopted a senior dog from a national rescue group. I'd be one of 17 million people who will adopt or purchase an animal this year. Why adopt? With all the animals sitting unwanted in cages, I can't justify buying from a breeder or pet store, and the breed doesn't really matter to me. I just want to give a dog a home and tons of love.

"There are so many wonderful animals in shelters," says Tori Fugate, director of marketing and communications for the Kansas City Pet Project in Missouri. "There's a misconception that the animals are there because they're broken, but that's not true. Often they come to us because their owners have moved or died, can no longer care for them, or just don't want them; it's through no fault of the pets." Mulling over adopting a canine companion? Keep these tips in mind:

FIND A SHELTER OR RESCUE GROUP
Shelters are often—not always—run by the local government and house all the animals in one facility. They accept animals on the spot, if necessary, and can adopt out the same day. They may or may not be no-kill, which means they don't euthanize animals

They need your help! About 1.2 million shelter dogs are put to sleep every year.

Very good dogs sometimes end up in shelters because their humans develop financial or health problems. Don't hold that against them!

unless there's a serious medical reason or they're dangerous. Rescue groups are privately run and nonprofit and usually keep animals in foster homes. They pull animals from shelters who are at risk of being euthanized due to space, age or behavior, or who have health issues. Some rescues are breed-specific. These groups generally have a more in-depth adoption process and charge more than a shelter does, due to the time and money invested in treating the dogs. If you want to know as much about your potential adoptee as possible, a rescue group will usually be your best option.

CONSIDER YOUR LIFESTYLE

Do you live in an apartment or a house? Have kids or roommates? Are you away from home for long stretches of the day? How active are you? "The shelter or rescue group will take this information into account when matching you with a dog," says Fugate. "We do play groups every day with dogs, so we know a lot about their behavior and energy level."

KNOW YOUR BUDGET

You may be able to find a dog for free, but shelters and rescues have significant expenses to cover—so expect to pay anywhere from $25 to $300 or more. In addition, you'll need to purchase food, bedding, toys, a leash and collar, a license and other products. Any unresolved or chronic medical issues, such as arthritis or skin conditions, can result in expenses on top of normal checkups and vaccinations. (Pet insurance can help with many vet costs, however it can run a couple hundred dollars a year or more.) All in all, you could easily spend several hundred dollars a year, excluding major medical expenses.

DO YOUR RESEARCH

Some communities have rules that prohibit certain breeds; commonly banned breeds include Rottweilers, bull terriers (aka pit bulls), mastiffs, Doberman pinschers, chow chows and bulldogs. While the ASPCA says there's no evidence that these types of laws reduce attacks on humans, they can make it difficult to legally license your dog. And check with your insurance company to make sure it doesn't have breed-specific rules for renters or homeowners. "If you're thinking about adopting a mixed-breed dog that may bear a resemblance to one of the above, bring a photo of it to your animal-control office to make sure it's allowed," says Fugate. (Note: Many towns are shifting to dangerous-dog ordinances, which focus on specific animals that have shown dangerous behavior, versus banning certain breeds entirely.)

CONSIDER FOSTERING

If you're not quite sure about your commitment level, consider adopting a senior (see "Better With

Better With Age

I'M A SUCKER FOR A GRAY muzzle, but not everyone is so enthusiastic about adopting a senior (generally any dog over the age of 7 or 8). People are afraid of increased cost for medications and vet bills, of lower energy levels—or simply that they won't get enough time with their dog before having to say goodbye. But loving a "vintage" model can be extremely rewarding. "They just have the biggest hearts, and they're often calmer," says Kansas City Pet Project's Tori Fugate. "All they want is a soft bed and to be comfortable and loved. And many of them don't need anything beyond your basic care."

If you're new to having a dog, adopting a senior can be a good way to get your feet wet, since you're not committing to 12 or more years of care. A rescue group (especially one that specializes in seniors) should be able to give you a better idea of any health issues a particular older dog may be facing.

Did you hear?
About 40 percent
of rescue dogs are
found through
word of mouth.

Not all rescue dogs are mutts (not that
there's anything wrong with that!): Up to
30 percent of shelter dogs are purebreds.

Age," page 89) or try fostering. "We call fostering 'dog dating,'" says Jme Thomas, founder and executive director of Motley Zoo Animal Rescue in Redmond, Washington. "It lets you flex your pet-ownership skills and will give you a good idea of how much your lifestyle will be impacted. We'd rather people give that a try than adopt a dog and give it up." It's not uncommon for foster parents to keep the dogs in their care; but some rescue groups won't allow it, since open foster homes allow them to get more animals out of the shelters. If you're interested, contact your local shelter or rescue group.

STAY IN TOUCH

While rescues tend to know their dogs well, it's no guarantee of smooth sailing. When I adopted my previous dog, who had been described as "goofy and loving," I soon discovered he had an aggressive side. The more secure he started to feel (and the more training and exercise I gave him), the more his goofy side came out—and the aggression faded. But I wish I had reached out to the group for help.

Good rescues and shelters will encourage you to stay in touch, especially if a dog isn't a good fit or you discover serious health or behavioral issues. Some adoption contracts will stipulate that you return the animal to the group (versus dropping it at a shelter or abandoning it) if there's a problem. —*Janet Lee* 🐾

Where to Look

BESIDES CHECKING WITH your local city, Humane Society or ASPCA shelter, these are some other places to launch your search.

1 **The Shelter Pet Project**
This nonprofit online pet-adoption website (in partnership with the Humane Society of the United States) lets you search nationwide for potential matches.

2 **Petfinder.com**
Another online pet-adoption website, this for-profit company features animals from shelters and rescue groups.

3 **Best Friends Animal Society**
This nonprofit, no-kill sanctuary has locations and network partners around the country.

4 **A Purposeful Rescue**
The Los Angeles–based nonprofit pulls dogs—often those with significant health problems that would put them high on a euthanasia list—from shelters, then sends them to fosters and finds them forever families. There are groups like this around the country.

HOW TO HELP YOUR DOG LIVE LONGER

Everything you need to know to improve your pet's health and add precious time to their life expectancy.

Dogs' lives are too short. Their only fault, really," says noted novelist Agnes Sligh Turnbull. It's unfortunately true: The average canine's life span is between 10 and 13 years, typically less for large breeds (as little as five years for the Dogue de Bordeaux) and more for smaller breeds, like the Chihuahua and Yorkshire terrier, who can live as long as 20 years. While science hasn't figured out how to permanently extend man's best friend's time here on Earth, there are a number of things owners can do to ensure that the years they do have are happy, healthy and as long as possible.

"We add dogs to our human families for companionship and unconditional love," notes veterinarian Natalie Marks, co-owner of Blum Animal Hospital in Chicago. "But, in return, we need to provide them with what they need for full physical and emotional health." Like humans, dogs require the most basic needs—food, water and shelter—but daily physical and mental exercise, like obedience training and brain-stimulating toys, are also essential for their overall well-being.

"A slow walk, where a pet can explore for 15 minutes, can wear him out as much as a 3-mile run," says Dr. Julie Reck.

Happy dogs tend to live longer because their bodies have less of the stress hormone cortisol, says Dr. Karen Becker.

HIGH-QUALITY FOOD

How much a dog should eat depends on its breed, size and age. But across the board, all should be given a high-quality food, whether it's dry, canned or raw, or if you choose to make it at home.

"There are so many choices in today's dog food market," notes Marks. "It's important to first make sure it is AAFCO [a dog food-certifying agency]-approved. Make sure it is life stage-appropriate (an all-life-stage food is actually formulated for a puppy and may not be appropriate for a senior). In addition, more and more research is coming out showing that grain-free diets are being linked to cardiomyopathies [potentially fatal diseases of the heart muscle]."

Veterinarian Karen Becker also suggests looking closely at the ingredients. Carbohydrates should make up less than 20 percent, and food should not contain synthetic nutrients, such as sulfates and oxides. "Look for a food that derives 99 percent or more of a pet's nutrients from real food, not lab-made vitamins."

REGULAR CHECKUPS

Whether your four-legged friend is a puppy, adult or senior, it's important to make regular trips to the veterinarian—and depending on its life stage, that could be more frequently than you'd think.

"Most of our puppies start to see the veterinarian between the ages of 6 and 9 weeks," explains Marks.

SEEING DOUBLE

The Controversy Over Cloning

WITH A LITTLE SCIENCE AND a lot of money, dog owners never really have to say goodbye. It all began in 2005, when a California woman paid $50,000 to clone her deceased dog using its DNA. In the years since then, the process has grown in popularity—but also in controversy. In order to create just one healthy genetic twin, multiple female dogs must undergo procedures to donate eggs and serve as the fertilized embryo's surrogate, living out their lives for the sole purpose of breeding—much like puppy mills—and inside a laboratory, no less.

And even if you do receive a successfully cloned version of your dog, there's no guarantee it will look or act identical to the original. Just ask Barbra Streisand, who had her 14-year-old Coton de Tulear, named Samantha, cloned in 2017, resulting in two puppies, Miss Violet and Miss Scarlett. "Each puppy is unique and has her own personality," the singer wrote in an op-ed piece for *The New York Times*. "You can clone the look of a dog, but you can't clone the soul."

"We then see them every three to four weeks, until they are finished with their vaccine series at around 16 weeks of age." Veterinarian Julie Reck adds, "In that first year, they will also need to be spayed or neutered."

Once a dog has reached adulthood, at around 16 months of age, vet visits should be made annually. "However, once a dog reaches around 8 years of age," notes Marks, "we strongly encourage semiannual wellness exams. Organ function and patient needs change more quickly at this stage of life, and it's important to have discussions and screen lab work more frequently."

EMOTIONAL HEALTH

Just like with humans, the mind can affect the body. It's essential to provide your pup with tools, such as mind-stimulating toys, positive-reinforcement training, medication, socialization or simply more exercise, to combat negative emotions. There are also online resources, like Fear Free (fearfreepets.com), an initiative with a mission to prevent and alleviate fear, anxiety and stress in pets by educating those who care for them.

"When dogs experience changes in their emotional health, we see behavioral changes such as separation anxiety, noise phobias and even reactivity [aggressive behaviors]," says Marks. "This is also one of the leading causes of relinquishment [to a shelter] and destruction of the human-animal bond. It's very important to talk to your veterinarian about how your dog exhibits signs of fear and anxiety so that it can be discussed, assessed and treated properly."

VITAMINS & SUPPLEMENTS

Pet wellness is a big trend right now, and there are scores of vitamins and supplements on the market: multivitamins; probiotics for healthy digestion; omega bites for shiny coats; and yummy-flavored chewable pills for allergy, joint and hip support. But does your pup really need these?

"If a dog is on a high-quality diet with daily exercise, an additional multivitamin is not necessary," explains Marks. "When dogs are diagnosed with certain disease conditions, like arthritis, heart disease or liver disease, there are supplements that add benefits.

"Some—such as milk thistle for liver health and regeneration, or glucosamine/chondroitin sulfate for joint health—have been proven to be effective in human and veterinary medicine," Marks continues. "However, others have only anecdotal support behind them and can be detrimental or contraindicated with some medical conditions or current medications."

GROOMING NEEDS

We brush our teeth every day, get regular haircuts and cut our nails when they grow too long— and canines require the same.

Dogs need the chance to get some exercise, even if it's just a walk, as often as they can.

"Regular grooming and nail trims are important to every dog's health and comfort," says Dr. Natalie Marks.

Grooming needs vary based on coat: Some should be brushed daily or weekly, while others rarely, if at all. Regardless of breed, every dog must have its nails trimmed every month or so, either with clippers or a battery-operated grinder. "Matted hair can cause secondary skin infections," explains Marks, "and overgrown nails can not only grow into the pad but can also cause lameness, increased risk for joint disease, and pain."

As for teeth, they should be brushed at least weekly (ideally, daily to keep tartar to a minimum)—and with a doggie toothbrush and toothpaste. Some pups may need to visit the vet for deeper cleanings, which can be done while they're sedated to make it stress-free. "Dental care is one of the best ways to increase the quality and quantity of a pet's life," explains Reck. "Once bacteria sets in under the gum line, it can easily enter the blood stream and cause infections in the heart and kidneys." According to Marks, dental disease is present in over 80 percent of dogs over the age of 3. "Not only is this a constant source of infection within the body," she says, "it can cause decreases in appetite, changes in behavior and be a source of pain."

While these are all activities most dogs don't enjoy, getting them accustomed to it from a young age helps, whether you do it at home (perhaps in the evenings, when the dog is most relaxed) or leave it to a professional groomer. 🐾

It won't get Rex high—but it might quell his anxiety.

CBD: Fact or Fad?

It's not just people who are enjoying the benefits of cannabidiol, aka CBD. In recent years, a growing number of canine products featuring CBD, a compound found in cannabis and hemp (not marijuana, which also contains psychoactive THC)—have become popular and are used to treat a host of issues, from anxiety and pain to epilepsy and cancer. "CBD products show encouraging promise in the treatment for many conditions in veterinary medicine, including arthritis and diseases related to anxiety such as lower urinary tract disease," explains Dr. Natalie Marks. "At this time, the use of these supplements is considered off-label and is still in clinical trials in the veterinary universities. However, the early results have veterinarians optimistic that it will be very helpful to many of our patients in the future." Possible side effects of CBD for dogs include dry mouth, lowered blood pressure and drowsiness. Always consult with your veterinarian before giving your pet CBD-based products.

When investing in dental products, go with those that have a Veterinary Oral Health Council seal on them, says Dr. Julie Reck.

Sometimes you have to ignore those puppy-dog eyes and keep your pet away from human food.

10 Things Your Dog Should Never Eat

A DOG BEGGING FOR table scraps can be hard to resist. And while the occasional bite of lean meat, carrots or eggs (cooked and not raw) is OK for most breeds, there are a handful of human goodies that will not only make your pup sick but could potentially be deadly. Before giving your dog anything that's not dog food or treats, always check with your veterinarian first—but under no circumstances should they be allowed to eat the following:

1
Chocolate
While milk and white chocolate are bad, dark and unsweetened chocolate are exponentially worse. If your dog eats any kind, it will suffer from diarrhea and vomiting, but a large amount can cause seizures and possibly death. Your vet should be contacted immediately.

2
Ice Cream
Milk and yogurt are mostly OK (although some pups can be lactose intolerant), but ice cream contains way too much sugar. However, there are lots of dog-friendly ice creams on the market that taste just as yummy!

3
Grapes & Raisins
Even a few of these can cause kidney failure. Excessive vomiting is an early warning sign that something is wrong.

4
Onions & Garlic
Like leeks and chives, they're poisonous (whether raw or cooked) —but garlic is five times more toxic. Symptoms can be delayed, so it's best to monitor your dog's health for a few days.

5
Coffee & Tea
Caffeine in any form, including coffee (also beans and grounds), tea, soda or energy drinks, can all be fatal.

6
Macadamia Nuts
While peanuts and peanut butter are safe, macadamias are an absolute no-no. Ingesting even just a few nuts can cause vomiting, lethargy, increased body temperature and weakness in the legs.

7
Avocado
The fruit contains persin, a toxin, and eating too much can cause vomiting or diarrhea.

8
Peaches & Plums
While most fruits, like slices of apples, bananas, oranges and watermelon, are safe, peaches and plums are troublesome because of their seeds, which contain cyanide.

9
Alcohol
This should go without saying, but if a dog ingests liquor, beer, wine or any food made with alcohol, it can cause vomiting, diarrhea, breathing problems, even death— and it's worse for smaller breeds.

10
Fat Trimmings & Bones
While your pet will likely be fine with a bite (as long as there's no seasoning), fat trimmed off the meat can cause inflammation of the pancreas. As for bones, they can splinter and block or cut the digestive system.

GOOD HEALTH

HOW DOGS HELP US HEAL

Our four-legged friends are more than mere companions.
They can also significantly help to boost our physical and mental health.

fter a bad day at the office— you made an error on a report, your boss scolded you and then you sat fuming in traffic during your commute home—there is often only one thing that can turn your mood around a full 180 degrees. And it's not a shot of whiskey or a glass of wine.

Rather, it's walking through the front door to be greeted by a happy, loving face that is excited to see you and clearly wants to spend time with you. Sure, your spouse or kid may also do this, but we're talking about your four-legged friend. How can you feel bad when your dog is jumping up, giving you kisses and is thrilled by the simple fact that you came home?

But there are also more benefits to owning a dog than just a quick mood boost after a lousy day. Researchers have discovered that having a canine in our lives goes a long way toward supporting both our mental and physical well-being. It may even add a few years to our lives.

"When you take good care of your dog, science shows, your dog is really good for you," says Steven Feldman, executive director of the Human Animal Bond Research Institute (HABRI). "I like to say that we eat our vegetables and get our exercise because we know they're part of being a healthy person. But there's another thing on that list [of health recommendations] that you might enjoy more, and that's owning a dog." Want proof? Here's what science says about how your dog may elevate your health.

DOGS AND FEEL-GOOD HORMONES

As any pet owner will tell you, taking care of an animal can be stressful. You may wake up in the middle of the night to use the bathroom and step into a puddle of dog vomit. Or, rather than going outside to relieve himself, your poodle may decide to use your in-laws' dining room rug when you visit. And then there is the anguish when your furry friend requires expensive medical care.

But overall, the positives far outweigh the negatives. "Everyone has a story about how pets have benefited them or a relative or a friend," Feldman says. "And we are starting to build the good, rigorous science behind that relationship people have with their pets."

According to a review of 69 studies published in 2012 in the journal *Frontiers in Psychology*, having a dog may decrease stress, anxiety and depression. Much of this is believed to be caused by a reduction in the hormone cortisol and in neurotransmitters such as epinephrine and norepinephrine— all of which play a role in stress.

At the same time as these negative factors decrease, there's an increase in the feel-good hormones prolactin (which is associated with nurturing) and endorphins (which are involved with the reward system in the brain). But the starring actor may be oxytocin, according to the *Frontiers in Psychology* review.

Stroking a dog for five to 24 minutes has been shown to increase levels of this so-called "love" or "cuddle" hormone in the bloodstream, and the effect is also greater if someone pets a familiar dog rather than a friendly yet unfamiliar dog, says study author Andrea Beetz, PhD, psychology professor at the University of Rostock in Germany. "In well-bonded human-dog relationships, even eye contact can lead to the release of oxytocin," she adds. In addition to reducing stress,

According to the American Heart Association, owning a pet (especially a dog), probably lowers the risk of cardiovascular disease.

Take time to stroke your dog a few times a day, and feel the stress melt away.

105

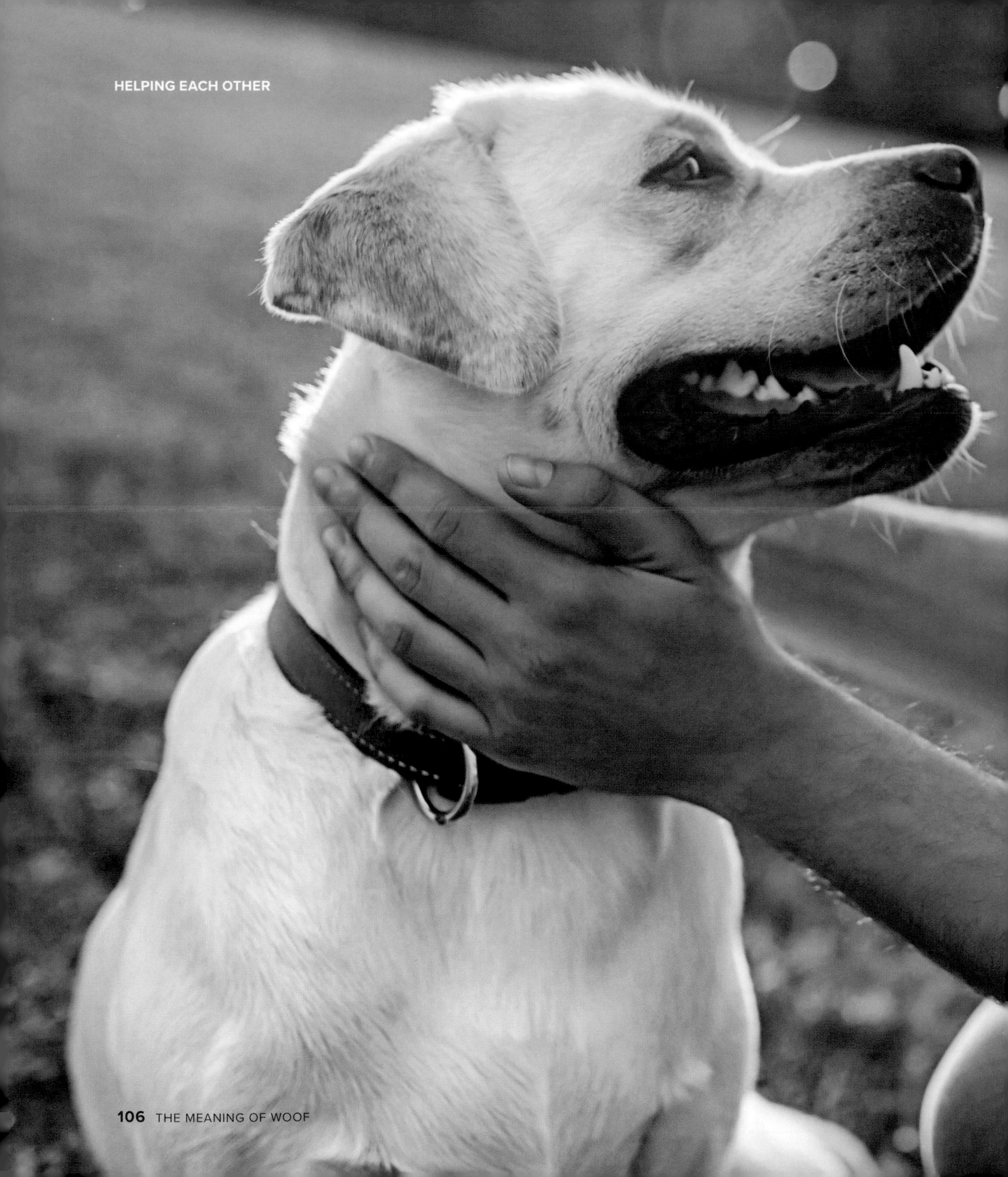

Both you and your pet see the benefits of increased oxytocin by spending time together.

Going to the Dogs

HUMAN-DOG INTERACTIONS aren't a one-way street—scientists are learning how our pets also benefit from spending quality time with us.

As in humans, levels of endorphins, prolactin and oxytocin increase in dogs with human contact, according to a 2014 review in *Animal Science and Biotechnology.* And a 2015 study published in the journal *Science* found that simply gazing into your pet's eyes increases levels of oxytocin in their brain— the same effect as when a mother gazes into her baby's eyes.

"The human-dog bond is similar to that of a parent and child, and oxytocin is really important in social relationships in many mammalian species," says Lauren Thielke, a PhD candidate at Oregon State University's Human-Animal Interaction Lab.

But what increased oxytocin means for your collie is still a mystery. Some have found that it increases affiliative behaviors, but others haven't re-created this in their work. Still, "overall, the dogs and the owners have higher oxytocin, which benefits dogs because it helps maintain that social bond so they have a good relationship with their owner," Thielke adds.

That is key. "If a companion animal isn't filling a relationship need for you, you may not get any benefit," notes Pamela Schreiner, PhD. And they likely won't either.

Unlike their wolf ancestors, dogs have evolved to produce pleasure hormones.

increased levels of oxytocin may also help alleviate fear and anxiety.

A survey conducted by HABRI found that 74 percent of pet owners reported having a pet helped to improve mental health. "Numerous studies have shown that rates of depression can be reduced with animals," says Feldman. And a study published in 2018 in *BMC Psychiatry* reported that pets are an effective way to help manage long-term mental health problems. "We've gone from thinking that it's nice to have a pet to realizing it may prove to be an essential way of coping with some mental health issues," adds Feldman.

A HEALTHIER HEART—AND MORE

Your head isn't the only thing that can benefit from having a dog. Studies show dog owners may also be physically healthier.

For one, research suggests that dog owners may get more physical activity than those who don't have canines. In a 2017 study of 3,100 adults, British scientists found that two-thirds of dog owners walked their pet at least once a day and, on average, were 20 percent more active than those without

a pooch. Dog owners were even less sedentary on days with the worst weather, compared to nonowners on days with the best weather conditions.

It's no wonder owning a dog has been linked with improved heart health. The American Heart Association released a statement in 2013 that said, "Pet ownership, particularly dog ownership, is probably associated with decreased cardiovascular disease risk."

In 2017, researchers explained why this may be true in a study published in the journal *Scientific Reports*.

The researchers looked at dogs and the risk of cardiovascular disease and death in 3.4 million people over a 12-year period. Those who owned a dog had a significantly lower risk of death from cardiovascular disease or other causes than nonowners. Single people with dogs saw the most benefit: a 33 percent decreased risk of death and 11 percent decreased risk of cardiovascular disease, compared to single people without dogs.

Scientists say there are several factors that help to explain why dogs may benefit your heart. In addition to prompting you to be

more physically active and exhibit less stress, having a pet may help your blood pressure return to normal levels more quickly following a stressful event.

Another theory is based on social support and a decrease in social isolation (a risk factor for cardiovascular disease). You have to walk your dog, and people tend to interact with you and your dog. "That builds," explains Pamela Schreiner, PhD, director of the Center to Study Human-Animal Relationships and Environments at the University of Minnesota. "As you are interacting with people and liking it, you start being more outgoing and seeking more interactions. Your dog is a vehicle for that—and helps you step outside of your own reticence."

PUPS AREN'T A MAGIC PILL

All these benefits are great reasons to get a dog. But owning a dog comes with a lot of responsibility. It's not all squeaky toys and games of fetch.

"Dogs need time and attention, and they cost money. For some people, it might be better to dog-sit for a few hours each week instead of having their own dog," Beetz says. Or consider volunteering at a shelter, walking dogs or simply playing with them; all can give you similar benefits. Dogs are good for you, but if you cannot properly care for a pet, they may add more stress—and nobody needs that. 🐾

> ## Dogs are tuned in to human emotions; they know when their family members are happy or sad, nervous or stressed.

If owning a pet isn't feasible, consider volunteering to walk dogs at a shelter. It'll be healthy for both of you.

Dogs are social—they need personal attention each day to thrive.

Depending on the age and breed, dogs should spend from 30 minutes to two hours being active each day.

More Things Dogs Can Do

THEY MAY NOT HAVE GONE TO med school, but dogs are helping us live longer, healthier lives. Here's a look at research-proven pups can make a difference.

● REDUCING ALLERGIES
Having early exposure to dogs and cats can help strengthen children's immune systems and curb their risk of developing asthma and eczema later in life. And even prenatal exposure to dogs can influence the development of a child's immune system, helping to minimize their risk of developing genetically linked allergies later in life, according to the Human Animal Bond Research Institute (HABRI).

● HELPING SENIORS
Therapy dogs can help to decrease agitated behaviors and increase social interactions in persons with dementia, notes HABRI. These pooches can also improve mood, function and quality of life in elderly dementia patients.

● REDUCING CHRONIC PAIN
A study of people with fibromyalgia found that 34 percent of patients reported some form of pain relief—plus improved mood and less fatigue—after spending 10 to 15 minutes with a therapy dog.

● KEEPING KIDS WITH CANCER COMPANY
The Canines and Childhood Cancer Study, sponsored by HABRI, has found dogs to have a calming effect on pediatric cancer patients, lowering blood pressure and heart rate.

● AIDING KIDS IN THE CLASSROOM
When dogs are present in a classroom, children are less likely to be aggressive and more likely to function on their own as well as improve emotional intelligence, according to HABRI.

● MAKING US ALL A LITTLE HAPPIER
The American Psychological Association reports that pet owners have greater self-esteem, are more conscientious and extroverted and tend to be less fearful.

PAWS FOR A CAUSE

The role of service dogs has evolved from guiding the blind to sensing low blood sugar, sniffing out food allergens and providing comfort.

O ver the past century, dogs have been trained for a number of jobs, providing service to those who have visual or hearing impairments, physical disabilities and mobility issues. And in recent years, their job description has grown to include impressive capabilities: assisting epileptics during seizures, sensing low blood sugar in diabetics, reminding a person with mental illness to take their medication, calming someone who suffers from PTSD, even detecting peanuts or gluten in food for those who suffer from life-threatening allergies.

Although "service dog" is the overarching term used to describe these special animals, there are a number of different classifications that specify the job for which they are trained (see "What Service Dogs Do," page 115).

Paws With a Cause, one of the leaders in the assistance-dog industry, excels at training seizure-response dogs. "Some dogs are taught to pull a personal alarm the client wears, when the client has a seizure in public," says Paws With a Cause public relations coordinator Cara Conway.

Therapy dogs are trained to bring comfort to others beyond their family members.

"They wear a waist leash, so the dog has to stay close when they're having a seizure and unconscious. Some of the other tasks our seizure-response dogs are taught to do are bracing to help the client get up after a seizure, retrieving a landline phone to call for help after a seizure, and making physical contact during a seizure to help bring the client out of it. After receiving a seizure-response dog, most of our clients regain the confidence they need to live a more active life."

Paws With a Cause also trains dogs for children with autism. While the dog provides comfort during stressful situations, it also performs physical tasks. "If the child has a tendency to bolt, they are tethered to the dog's harness," says Conway. "When the child starts to bolt, the parent tells the dog to 'stop,' which in turn stops the child. This one simple task gives parents the freedom to take their child out in public without fear of their running into a dangerous situation."

Many service dogs give their all to those who did the same for their country. According to the National Center for PTSD, some 11 to 20 percent of military veterans have post-traumatic stress disorder, with 22 vets committing suicide every day. To help ease their struggles, many organizations pair service dogs with those suffering from a variety of war-related issues—both physical and mental—at no cost, thanks to generous donations. Freedom Service Dogs in Denver, which trains dogs rescued from shelters, offers two such programs, Operation Freedom and Operation Full Circle, which help returning war veterans and military personnel transition from active duty and combat to civilian life. "These dogs can be trained to provide emotional support, interrupt flashbacks, provide pressure therapy and do more physical tasks, such as checking out a room, posting up in front of their client, and waking clients from nightmares," explains Erin Conley, Freedom Service Dogs director of communications.

The programs don't just benefit veterans, though. Some organizations utilize nonviolent inmates to train the dogs—who live in their prison cells until they graduate—like America's VetDogs Prison Puppy Program. "The inmate is able to give back to society, to make the life of a veteran better as well as learning how to train service dogs, which can be a valuable life skill," explains John Miller, president and CEO.

While service dogs are protected under the 1990 Americans With Disabilities Act, granting them full public access with their handlers, another genre of canine companions doesn't yet qualify. According to the ADA, therapy, crisis-response and emotional-support dogs "provide comfort just by being with a person" and are not trained to perform a task for the disabled, like service dogs are. Still, some local and state laws allow them in places where they are normally prohibited, such as on public transportation and in stores and restaurants.

Certified therapy dogs may not be considered service dogs, but their role is no less important. These sweet souls provide comfort at hospitals, in nursing homes, in hospices, in disaster areas and in schools. In a growing trend, funeral homes are offering grief-therapy dogs. Judd, a 4-year-old golden retriever, is so popular at Armes-Hunt Funeral Home in Fairmount, Indiana, he has his own Facebook page filled with thank-you messages from mourners he's helped over the years. "He provides comfort and compassion during a difficult time of loss," explains Judd's handler, Shari Wallace. "He amazes me every day with the gift he has of meeting people right where they need him to be, in a way no human could ever touch. We call him our four-legged angel."

Smart and gentle, Golden and Labrador retrievers are among the most popular choices for service dogs.

What Service Dogs Do

● **GUIDE DOG**
Assists the visually impaired

● **HEARING DOG**
Alerts the hearing-impaired to sounds, such as a telephone, doorbell, smoke alarm or a crying baby

● **MOBILITY DOG**
Helps handler walk or keep their balance while in motion in addition to retrieving items, opening doors or pushing buttons for them

● **MEDICAL ALERT/MEDICAL RESPONSE DOG**
Warns about oncoming medical conditions, such as a seizure or low blood sugar, and assists in the event of epilepsy, stroke or heart attack by breaking handler's fall with its body or seeking help from humans

● **PSYCHIATRIC SERVICE DOG**
Works with those who have a mental disability, including disorders such as PTSD, depression and anxiety, by calming them—and can be trained to remind handler to take prescribed medication

● **AUTISM SERVICE DOG**
Nurtures handler's independence, whether that means providing comfort and focus during stressful times or aiding in social settings

Training a service dog can take anywhere from six to nine months, depending on a client's needs.

More than 30 percent of the University of British Columbia's student body takes advantage of the B.A.R.K. program.

Campus Canines

STRESSED-OUT COLLEGE students find comfort with canine-therapy programs.

College can be an anxious time. To ease the pressure, a growing number of schools (at least 925, in the U.S.), including Yale, Dartmouth, Tufts, Occidental and Oberlin, are providing aid to students with on-campus canine-therapy programs. At the University of British Columbia, associate professor John-Tyler Binfet, PhD, has established B.A.R.K. (Building Academic Retention through K9s)—one of the largest programs, with 60 dog-handler teams who do weekly drop-ins in addition to staffing stations throughout the campus where students are welcome to spend time with a pup and relax. Each year, more than 4,000 take advantage of B.A.R.K., with the average person staying 35 minutes at a time.

"Our mission in B.A.R.K. is to reduce stress and homesickness in students and to foster connections among students so they feel supported on campus," explains Binfet, who was inspired after he saw the reaction to his dog, Frances. "We know students who feel socially and emotionally supported do better academically.... As a researcher, it's really gratifying work, and I regularly hear from students just how meaningful B.A.R.K. is to them. They often tell me they chose our campus because of the dog-therapy program, or that the dogs kept them on campus during troubling times, when they perhaps thought being a university student was too tough."

PART 4

FIND YOUR PERFECT MATCH

Whether it's a rare breed or a popular one, there's a type of dog to suit every need and personality.

193 American Kennel Club Breeds

ABOUT EACH BREED

Learn more about the characteristics, temperament, care and history of each breed recognized by the American Kennel Club.

Welcoming a dog into your family is definitely rewarding, but it's also a major commitment and a life-changing responsibility. When selecting a pet that is the best fit for your lifestyle, there are a number of criteria to take into consideration: Do you work long hours? Live in a small space? Have young children? Does anyone have allergies? A breed's size, temperament, activity level, trainability and more are all important factors to keep in mind when researching the most compatible pup for you.

For some dogs though, looks can be deceiving. While the greyhound is the fastest breed and synonymous with racing, it's often referred to as the 40-mph couch potato—meaning it prefers a comfy bed to a big backyard. Another misconception is that dogs with thick coats, like the Alaskan malamute or Siberian husky, must live in cold climates. And it's not just large breeds that make good watchdogs. The toy poodle, which maxes out at 6 pounds, is rated as one of the best protectors of the home.

While there are more than 400 different dog breeds in the world, including designer dogs like the goldendoodle and puggle (turn to page 180 for more on the popular mixed breeds), the American Kennel Club officially recognizes approximately 200 retrievers, sight hounds, scent hounds, spaniels, herders and terriers. Read on to learn about them all and find your ideal four-legged best friend!

A

Afghan Hound

Airedale Terrier

Akita

Affenpinscher

Affenpinscher
🏅 Canine Comedian
AKC Breed Popularity No. 148
Temperament Confident, famously funny, fearless
Average Size 9-11.5 inches, 7-10 pounds **Activity Level** Average
Shedding Seasonal **Trainability** Easy
Life Expectancy 12-15 years

Quite the humanlike breed, the affenpinscher amuses with both its appearance and personality. The sturdy, compact dog has a wiry coat, and the hair on its head is usually brushed over the eyes. In the 1600s, they were bred to exterminate rats by day and be bed warmers at night. Because of this, these terriers don't do well in homes where rodents are kept as pets. Affenpinschers are so smart, just basic obedience training is recommended, but keep the sessions short yet frequent. If you think the affenpinscher is right for you, have some patience, since the breed is so rare—although, arguably, this silly little dog is worth the wait!

Afghan Hound
🏅 Most Elegant
AKC Breed Popularity No. 113
Temperament Independent, sweet
Average Size 25-27 inches, 50-60 pounds **Activity Level** Energetic **Shedding** Infrequent
Trainability May be stubborn
Life Expectancy 12-18 years

There's no canine more aristocratic-looking than the Afghan hound. Its defining feature, a thick silky coat, is not just for show: Thousands of years ago, it offered protection from the harsh climates of the mountain regions in what is now Afghanistan. Under its glorious coat is a svelte physique accented by protruding hipbones—a characteristic of the agile sight hound, not a sign of being underweight. But don't let the breed's unparalleled beauty fool you—this loyal dog can be silly or aloof.

Airedale Terrier
🏅 Most Versatile
AKC Breed Popularity No. 60
Temperament Friendly, clever, courageous **Average Size** 23 inches, 50-70 pounds **Activity Level** Average

Shedding Occasional **Trainability** Eager to please **Life Expectancy** 11-14 years

The "king of the terriers" is highly alert, strong, athletic and rambunctious, so it's important to give it multiple walks and play sessions daily. Also, because of its size, activity level and stubbornness, obedience training is recommended. Despite its high energy, the breed can still be patient with small children and excels in family activities—proving the Airedale is a truly versatile dog.

Akita
🏅 Family Protector
AKC Breed Popularity No. 47
Temperament Courageous, dignified, profoundly loyal **Average Size** 26-28 inches, 70-130 pounds **Activity Level** Energetic **Shedding** Seasonal **Trainability** Eager to please
Life Expectancy 10-13 years

If you're seeking a courageous dog to safeguard your home, look no further than the Akita. The large breed is not only muscular and

American English Coonhound

powerful, but also hardwired to protect its family. Because of its stature and instincts, it's vital that Akitas be trained from puppyhood and socialized to be familiar with strangers. The breed can be aggressive toward other dogs, particularly those of the same sex, so use extreme caution during all canine interactions. Additionally, Akitas can be food-possessive and should only be fed away from other animals and children. Despite their size, Akitas do well in small homes, as long as they receive sufficient daily exercise, such as a brisk walk around the block.

Alaskan Malamute
♀ Hard Worker
AKC Breed Popularity No. 58
Temperament Affectionate, loyal, playful **Average Size** 23-25 inches, 75-85 pounds **Activity Level** Energetic **Shedding** Seasonal **Trainability** Independent **Life Expectancy** 10-14 years

Despite its name, the Alaskan Malamute doesn't require a cold climate—but it does need to burn

Alaskan Malamute

DID YOU KNOW?
In 2010, the Malamute became the state dog of Alaska, after a campaign started by schoolchildren.

off a lot of energy, whether that's running around a yard, hiking or swimming. An inherent trait is its desire to be a pack animal; obedience training as a puppy is a must so that it learns to respect its owner as the leader. Once it's trained, you'll have a well-behaved dog who's great with kids.

American English Coonhound
♀ Spirited Hunter
AKC Breed Popularity No. 175
Temperament Sweet, mellow, sociable **Average Size** 23-26 inches, 45-65 pounds **Activity Level** Energetic **Shedding** Occasional **Trainability** Agreeable **Life Expectancy** 11-12 years

The sleek and muscular breed was created in the 1800s to hunt raccoons, so be aware that its instinctive prey drive remains: The sight hound should never be off-leash in an unsecured area. Because of its strong endurance, the dog is ideal for anyone who wants a running or hiking partner, as it needs lots of exercise to stay happy and healthy. At home though, the American English coonhound is quite mellow.

American Eskimo Dog

American Eskimo Dog
♀ Beauty & Brains
AKC Breed Popularity No. 122
Temperament Playful, perky, smart **Average Size** 9-12 inches, 6-10 pounds (toy); 12-15 inches, 10-20 pounds (miniature); 15-19 inches, 25-35 pounds (standard) **Activity Level** Energetic **Shedding** Seasonal **Trainability** Eager to please **Life Expectancy** 13-15 years

A total package, the American Eskimo dog is as smart as it is striking. The breed comes in three sizes (toy, miniature and standard), each with the same distinct features: fluffy white coat, smiling face and intelligent expression. The clever breed is also one of the easiest to train and should be given stimulating toys and mental challenges, because a bored Eskie is a destructive Eskie. An indoor dog, it craves companionship and is happiest at home, interacting with the family it loves—which means it should not be left alone for long periods of time, or behavioral problems can develop. Its sparkly coat is surprisingly easy to keep clean; just be sure to brush it multiple times a week to prevent matting and excessive shedding.

American Foxhound

🏅 **Loudest Voice**

AKC Breed Popularity No. 186
Temperament Independent, easygoing, sweet **Average Size** 21-25 inches, 60-70 pounds
Activity Level Energetic **Shedding** Seasonal **Trainability** Independent
Life Expectancy 11-13 years

Beloved by Founding Fathers George Washington and Thomas Jefferson, the American foxhound is as old as the country for which it is named. Just like any scent hound, it's renowned for its speed, endurance and work ethic. But it was specifically bred to chase prey for hours—and that characteristic requires lots of daily exercise (at least an hour or two—and never off-leash) so the dog doesn't become bored and destructive. Potential owners should also know the American foxhound's "voice" is a loud bawling that can carry for miles. To prevent that from becoming a nuisance for you and your neighbors, obedience training is recommended at a very young age. A well-adjusted foxhound is mild-tempered and good with children.

American Hairless Terrier

American Staffordshire Terrier

American Water Spaniel

Anatolian Shepherd Dog

American Foxhound

American Hairless Terrier

🏅 **Allergy-Friendly**

AKC Breed Popularity No. 136
Temperament Energetic, alert, curious **Average Size** 12-16 inches, 12-16 pounds **Activity Level** Average **Shedding** Seasonal **Trainability** Eager to please
Life Expectancy 14-16 years

Despite its name, the American hairless terrier comes in both hair-free and coated varieties. The hairless version is one of the best breeds for those who suffer from allergies. But its skin also requires special care: Sunburn is a concern, so apply sunscreen whenever the dog is outdoors. Speaking of which, the American hairless terrier needs only moderate daily exercise, be it from playing with people or other dogs in a fenced-in yard or taking a walk around the block. Inside, the intelligent and easy-to-train breed is protective of its family and makes a good watchdog—when it's not curled up on the couch.

American Staffordshire Terrier

🏅 **Loyal Friend**

AKC Breed Popularity No. 85
Temperament Playful, alert, sensitive **Average Size** 17-19 inches, 40-70 pounds **Activity Level** Average **Shedding** Occasional **Trainability** Agreeable
Life Expectancy 12-16 years

Don't be tricked by its muscular build: The American Staffordshire terrier is incredibly agile and graceful, with a mellow personality. Still, the athletic breed is high energy and requires a lot of daily exercise. And because the AmStaff is so people-oriented, activity should involve interacting with its owner rather than running around the yard by itself. Due to its great strength and exuberance, the AmStaff should also receive obedience training as early as puppyhood, although behaviors like chewing and digging may be hard to break. While the breed is good-natured in general and loyal to its human family, even the most socialized AmStaff should never be left alone with other dogs.

American Water Spaniel
🏅 **Expert Swimmer**

AKC Breed Popularity No. 166
Temperament Eager, happy, charming **Average Size** 15-18 inches, 25-45 pounds **Activity Level** Average **Shedding** Infrequent **Trainability** Eager to please **Life Expectancy** 10-14 years

As its name suggests, the American water spaniel loves to swim, which it can do like a seal, thanks to thickly padded feet and webbed toes. But the breed fares just as well on land and enjoys a variety of outdoor sports, like hunting. Physical activity, especially with its owner, is the key to the athletic dog's mental and emotional health and should at least include daily vigorous play. The American water spaniel thrives when given a job, but if that's not as a hunting companion, field or agility competitions will also do the trick.

Anatolian Shepherd Dog
🏅 **Devoted Guardian**

AKC Breed Popularity No. 90
Temperament Loyal, independent, reserved **Average Size** 27-29 inches, 80-150 pounds **Activity Level** Average **Shedding** Seasonal **Trainability** Independent **Life Expectancy** 11-13 years

The Anatolian shepherd dog dates back more than 6,000 years, to the Bronze Age; but the smart and rugged breed has remained timeless and mostly unchanged. Originally bred to protect livestock, its instincts translate to its family—including canine members—although due to its calm demeanor, it would rather intimidate predators than fight them. The only downside to the dog's independence and intensity is the challenge of obedience training, which is a must for the dominating breed, so owners need to be firm in their approach. Despite its large size, the Anatolian needs only moderate exercise, like one or two daily walks, as long as it's always kept on-leash.

Australian Cattle Dog
🏅 **Doggie Genius**

AKC Breed Popularity No. 55
Temperament Alert, curious, sensitive **Average Size** 17-20 inches, 35-50 pounds **Activity Level** Energetic **Shedding** Regular **Trainability** May be stubborn **Life Expectancy** 12-16 years

A resilient herder with a strong work drive, the Australian cattle dog is so intelligent, owners need to stay on their toes to make sure they're not outsmarted. Although the breed, also known as the blue heeler, is happiest when on the job, there are a number of activities, like agility training or daily runs, that can keep the active dog physically and mentally fit. The ACD's coat is double layered but

Australian Cattle Dog

low-maintenance, with little to no odor, so an occasional bath will keep it smelling fresh.

Australian Shepherd
🏅 **Most Energetic**

AKC Breed Popularity No. 15
Temperament Smart, work-oriented, exuberant **Average Size** 20-23 inches, 50-65 pounds (male); 18-21 inches, 40-55 pounds (female) **Activity Level** Energetic **Shedding** Seasonal **Trainability** Eager to please **Life Expectancy** 12-15 years

Driven by a tireless desire to herd and guard, the Australian shepherd is one of the most intelligent working dogs. Off-duty, it will still exhibit those instincts with its family's children and pets. Aussies also have boundless energy and stamina, which may not be ideal for all potential owners—especially those who aren't active. But if the breed appeals to you, keep in mind: It's important to channel its exuberance into agility training or working as a therapy or service dog, which it can pick up easily, due to its keen intelligence. The loyal Aussie is so overprotective that if left alone for too long, it can become destructive.

15th MOST POPULAR BREED!

Australian Shepherd

B

Australian Terrier

Best Personality

AKC Breed Popularity No. 139 **Temperament** Affectionate, courageous, spirited **Average Size** 10–11 inches, 15–20 pounds **Activity Level** Energetic **Shedding** Infrequent **Trainability** Agreeable **Life Expectancy** 11–15 years

A big personality is packed into the smart, outgoing and confident Australian terrier's little body. Despite its size, the dog will act as a devoted guardian of its home, because it feels it's a true member of the family. To that end, the people-oriented breed must be treated as such—and not have to share your love (or its toys) with another dog—or it will feel neglected and act out. A true terrier, it loves to dig. But don't worry: Its waterproof coat repels dirt, so it's easy to maintain.

Basenji

Quietest

AKC Breed Popularity No. 87 **Temperament** Independent, smart, poised **Average Size** 16–17 inches, 22–24 pounds **Activity Level** Energetic **Shedding** Occasional **Trainability** Independent **Life Expectancy** 13–14 years

For anyone opening up their home to a dog for the first time, the sweet-faced Basenji is an attractive option. Considered a catlike canine, the breed not only doesn't bark (they make a sound that's more like a yodel), but it also lacks any "doggie" smell. It's fairly active and inquisitive, and requires a lot of regular exercise. Without it, the Basenji will become bored, which can lead to destructive behavior. Given the breed's mischievous side, puppy-training classes are necessary—and will have a greater effect when the atmosphere is encouraging and rewarding.

Basset Hound

Laziest

AKC Breed Popularity No. 39 **Temperament** Charming, patient, low-key **Average Size** Up to 15 inches, 40–65 pounds **Activity Level** Calm **Shedding** Occasional **Trainability** Independent **Life Expectancy** 12–13 years

"Stubborn and slow-moving, with adorably-droopy eyes" perfectly sums up the charm of the basset hound. Unlike others bred to hunt, this low-slung dog relies on the accuracy of its nose rather than speed and agility to get the job done. At home, the basset hound is happiest spending its day napping. But while not as active as most other breeds, it does require some exercise—at the very least, a daily walk around the neighborhood to interact with doggie friends (and keep it from becoming overweight)—before heading straight back to sleep once home again.

Beagle

Happy-Go-Lucky

AKC Breed Popularity No. 6 **Temperament** Friendly, curious, merry **Average Size** 13–15 inches, 20–30 pounds **Activity Level**

Basset Hound

Bearded Collie

Beauceron

Energetic **Shedding** Seasonal **Trainability** Agreeable **Life Expectancy** 10-15 years

As cute as it is happy, the beagle has been one of the most popular breeds for years. Loving, loyal and clever, it's an excellent pet that thrives on companionship, whether with humans or another dog in the home. The scent hound, well-known for its musical bark, requires a good deal of activity, at least an hour a day, to balance its energy. Not only should walks be on-leash, but outdoor romps need to be secure, as beagles are escape artists: Fencing should be at least 5 feet high and extend underground to prevent tunneling.

Bearded Collie
✪ Best Facial Hair
AKC Breed Popularity No. 127 **Temperament** Smart, bouncy, charismatic **Average Size** 20-22 inches, 45-55 pounds **Activity Level** Average **Shedding** Seasonal **Trainability** Independent **Life Expectancy** 12-14 years

As its name implies, the bearded collie has quite a unique look—one that is easy to love, but it does come with some upkeep. Every day, the shaggy breed must be brushed to remove tangles; every week, a comb should be used (along with anti-tangle spray) to remove dead hair, which could take up to an hour. Still, beardie enthusiasts say it's well worth the effort for such a charismatic, friendly, affectionate dog. Also rambunctious, it loves outdoor activities, no matter the weather, and would be best suited to an owner who's game for a jog or hike (or, at the very least, throwing a ball in the yard) all year long.

Beauceron
✪ Brains & Brawn
AKC Breed Popularity No. 124 **Temperament** Gentle, faithful, obedient **Average Size** 24-28 inches, 70-110 pounds **Activity Level** Energetic **Shedding** Frequent **Trainability** Easy **Life Expectancy** 10-12 years

A breed that's been revered for centuries for its intelligence, power and strong work ethic, the Beauceron is not for the novice dog owner (or one who does not exhibit dominance). If not "working" as a herder, it will require other physical and mental challenges to channel that intensity. Yet for someone who enjoys a variety of outdoor activities, the breed is a perfect match. Easy to train, the Beauceron is an endearing and loyal dog that will proudly serve as its family's protector and is especially good with small children.

Bedlington Terrier
✪ Least Likely to Shed
AKC Breed Popularity No. 141 **Temperament** Loyal, charming, frolicking **Average Size** 15-17.5 inches, 17-23 pounds **Activity Level** Energetic **Shedding** Infrequent **Trainability** Agreeable **Life Expectancy** 11-16 years

The saying "wolf in sheep's clothing" can be used to describe the Bedlington terrier—the hunting dog looks like a little lamb! And its personality is just as sweet. A ball of energy and fun, it loves nothing more than being the center of its family's attention, which it will repay by being a fierce protector. And while the Bedlington is quite lively, playing in the yard or on a long walk, once back home, the dog is relaxed and perfectly happy to cuddle up on the couch. Even better: The Bedlington terrier does not shed, making it one of the most ideal hypoallergenic breeds.

Bedlington Terrier

Belgian Malinois
✦ World-Class Worker
AKC Breed Popularity No. 43
Temperament Confident, smart, hardworking **Average Size** 22-26 inches, 40-80 pounds
Activity Level Energetic **Shedding** Seasonal **Trainability** Easy
Life Expectancy 14-16 years

Similar in appearance and disposition to the German shepherd but less well known, the Belgian Malinois has served with distinction as a police and military K-9 officer for years. Athletic yet elegant, the breed requires a good amount of physical and mental activity—and it must be with its owner. The Belgian Malinois is exceedingly devoted to its human companion and will forge an unbreakable bond that quite literally gives the dog its reason for being. Due to the breed's high prey drive, it's imperative that it receive obedience training as early as possible. Don't be surprised if the puppy is at the head of its class: Because of the Belgian Malinois' intelligence, it will pick up commands quickly and easily.

Belgian Sheepdog
✦ Most Passionate
AKC Breed Popularity No. 125
Temperament Bright, watchful, serious-minded **Average Size** 22-26 inches, 45-75 pounds
Activity Level Energetic **Shedding** Seasonal **Trainability** Easy
Life Expectancy 12-14 years

Much like the Belgian Malinois, the dog is a sensitive soul who craves human companionship. The versatile Belgian sheepdog gives 100 percent, no matter the task, whether it's K-9 duty, protecting the home or simply fetching a ball. And it needs someone who's equally dedicated, since the breed requires lots of exercise—ideally, with its owner, to whom it's deeply bonded.

Belgian Tervuren
✦ Do-It-All Dog
AKC Breed Popularity No. 106
Temperament Courageous, alert, intelligent **Average Size** 22-26 inches, 45-75 pounds **Activity Level** Energetic **Shedding** Seasonal **Trainability** Easy
Life Expectancy 12-14 years

Slightly more popular than the Belgian sheepdog, it's also a tireless worker, whether herding livestock or protecting the family. The super-intelligent breed truly loves nothing more than to master a task, especially if it pleases its owner. But it's not all work and no play for the Belgian Tervuren. In fact, the affectionate dog delights in spending time with its human and particularly enjoys participating in activities together.

Bergamasco Sheepdog
✦ Social Butterfly
AKC Breed Popularity No. 184
Temperament Independent, sociable, intelligent **Average Size** 22-23.5 inches, 51-84 pounds **Activity Level** Calm **Shedding** Infrequent **Trainability** Agreeable **Life Expectancy** 13-15 years

With a look this eye-catching, the Bergamasco sheepdog commands attention—and as a highly sociable breed, it relishes it. The loving and protective Bergamasco will develop independent relationships with every member of its family and relate to them in an individual way. Despite its matted coat, which is comprised of three types of hair, the breed is low-maintenance and needs to be bathed only a few times a year. Another surprise: the Bergamasco doesn't shed and is hypoallergenic for those allergic to dogs. However, people with allergies to wool or lanolin have been known to show symptoms.

Berger Picard
🏅 **Best Workout Buddy**
AKC Breed Popularity No. 144
Temperament Loyal, good-natured, observant **Average Size** 21.5-25.5 inches, 50-70 pounds
Activity Level Energetic **Shedding** Seasonal **Trainability** Easy
Life Expectancy 12-13 years

An athletic dog with lots of stamina, the Berger Picard is an ideal companion for active people. For the breed, daily exercise is a must to keep it healthy and happy. At least one long walk a day is expected, but the Berger Picard also enjoys swimming, playing fetch, hiking and running alongside its owner during a jog or bike ride. Because of its stubborn nature, early training is necessary but will be fairly easy, thanks to the breed's intelligence.

Berger Picard

Bernese Mountain Dog

Bernese Mountain Dog
🏅 **Most Powerful**
AKC Breed Popularity No. 22
Temperament Gentle, independent, noble **Average Size** 23-27.5 inches, 70-115 pounds **Activity Level** Energetic **Shedding** Frequent
Trainability Independent
Life Expectancy 7-10 years

Most working breeds are quite strong, but none is as powerful as the Bernese mountain dog. With its broad and muscular hind quarters, it's able to pull many times its own weight when hauling a cart. The Bernese mountain dog is also as beautiful as it is brawny, with a sweet, affectionate disposition to boot. Always eager to please, it will get along with the whole family (and be especially gentle with small children), although one lucky member will probably hold the key to the dog's heart.

Bichon Frise
🏅 **Impossibly Cute**
AKC Breed Popularity No. 46
Temperament Playful, curious, peppy **Average Size** 9.5-11.5 inches, 12-18 pounds **Activity Level** Average **Shedding** Infrequent **Trainability** Agreeable **Life Expectancy** 14-15 years

Much more than just a "little white dog," the bichon frise is amusing, charming, clever and loving—which explains why it was the favored breed of Spanish, Italian and French royalty for centuries. All these years later, it's still delighting owners, with a merry temperament that's written all over its adorable powder-puff face (and evidenced by the literal pep in its step). Although notoriously difficult to housebreak, the breed is easy to train...to perform tricks. The bichon frise is also quite adaptable: It will get along with other dogs and children and, thanks to its confidence, will even do nicely living in the city. And for all that poofy fur (which should be brushed daily), it sheds very little and is actually hypoallergenic.

Bichon Frise

Black and Tan Coonhound

♀ All-American Dog

AKC Breed Popularity No. 138
Temperament Easygoing, bright, brave **Average Size** 23-27 inches, 65-110 pounds **Activity Level** Average
Shedding Seasonal
Trainability Independent
Life Expectancy 10-12 years

The appropriately named black and tan coonhound is a dog bred to hunt raccoons and has a coal-black coat and tan "pumpkin seed"-looking markings above its eyes. But it still makes an excellent pet, even if not used for that purpose. Sociable, intelligent, sweet and friendly, the B&T adores its family and enjoys spending lots of time with them. Just keep in mind: It's a hound through and through—and perhaps to a fault. The B&T's instinct to hunt is always active, even if prey is nowhere in sight; its sensitive nose can pick up on the faintest scent, meaning that the dog must always be walked on a leash and its yard should have a tall, strong fence.

Black and Tan Coonhound

Bloodhound

Black Russian Terrier

Black Russian Terrier

♀ Super Dog

AKC Breed Popularity No. 118
Temperament Intelligent, calm, powerful **Average Size** 26-30 inches, 80-130 pounds
Activity Level Energetic
Shedding Seasonal **Trainability** Easy
Life Expectancy 10-12 years

Nicknamed the "Black Pearl of Russia," the BRT is a powerful and tireless worker that originally patrolled Soviet borders and Joseph Stalin's notorious prison camps. The dog was bred to guard and protect, and the courage and confidence it possesses is still as instinctive today. But those traits also must be managed, with proper training beginning in puppyhood. Without it, the Black Russian terrier will become pushy and dominating with anyone it can control. Similarly, if the breed doesn't get enough exercise—at least 30 minutes a day—it will act out and be destructive. And at 100-plus pounds, that can be a lot of damage.

Bloodhound

♀ Best Nose

AKC Breed Popularity No. 49
Temperament Friendly, independent, inquisitive **Average Size** 23-27 inches, 90-110 pounds **Activity Level** Average **Shedding** Seasonal **Trainability** Independent **Life Expectancy** 10-12 years

Technology has yet to invent anything that rivals the accuracy of the bloodhound's nose. The world-famous "sleuth hound" has the uncanny ability to find humans who are lost or hiding from police, based only on their scent. Even off-duty, the breed, which tends to drool, is still on its game, and a strong leash is always recommended; the bloodhound—otherwise docile and easygoing—won't give up the hunt until the trail ends, even if it's hours later. Proper training early on can offset this behavior, although with a stubborn dog, that too can be challenging. Just remain patient and firm (and reward the pup with lots of treats and praise).

Bluetick Coonhound
🏅 **Best Cold Nose**

AKC Breed Popularity No. 130
Temperament Smart, devoted, tenacious **Average Size** 21-27 inches, 45-80 pounds **Activity Level** Energetic **Shedding** Seasonal **Trainability** Agreeable **Life Expectancy** 11-12 years

No matter how old the scent, the bluetick coonhound and its "cold nose" will work it until the end. The breed is relentless in its quest, but if the dog is a pet (and not working), its off-the-charts prey drive must be managed with obedience training (plus a strong leash). As a hunting dog, the bluetick does require plenty of daily exercise, but once inside the home and surrounded by the family it so deeply loves, the breed is just as happy to peacefully nap.

DID YOU KNOW?
Since 1953, the bluetick coonhound has been the mascot for the University of Tennessee.

Boerboel
🏅 **Most Territorial**

AKC Breed Popularity No. 121
Temperament Confident, intelligent, calm **Average Size** 22-27 inches, 150-200 pounds **Activity Level** Average **Shedding** Occasional **Trainability** Agreeable **Life Expectancy** 9-11 years

Not for the novice dog owner, the Boerboel is a massive and domineering breed, obsessed with protecting the family it adores and their home. Because of the Boerboel's size and territorial disposition, it's imperative that obedience training begin immediately as a puppy, when it's most easygoing and impressionable, and that it remain consistent and long-term well into adulthood. A happy and healthy Boerboel is intelligent, loyal, confident, eager to learn and, above all, devoted to its human companions, making it an ideal watchdog.

Boerboel

Bluetick Coonhound

Most Popular Dog Names

Just like with babies, dog names follow trends. Over the past few years, pop culture has served as a strong influence—from sci-fi villains Loki, Thanos and Anakin to Fortnite video-game characters, even members of the royal family (George, Charlotte, Harry and Meghan have all grown in popularity). There's also been an uptick in owners finding inspiration from their favorite foods and drinks: Biscuit, Waffles, Whiskey and Guinness are on the rise as well. Need some help naming your new pup? According to research conducted by Rover, the world's largest network of pet sitters and dog walkers, these are the 20 most popular right now!

Top 10 Female Names

1	Bella	6	Sadie
2	Luna	7	Molly
3	Lucy	8	Bailey
4	Daisy	9	Stella
5	Lola	10	Maggie

Top 10 Male Names

1	Max	6	Rocky
2	Charlie	7	Duke
3	Cooper	8	Bear
4	Buddy	9	Tucker
5	Jack	10	Oliver

Border Terrier

Border Collie

Boston Terrier

Borzoi

Border Collie
♛ Best All-Around

AKC Breed Popularity No. 35
Temperament Affectionate, smart, energetic **Average Size** 18-22 inches, 30-55 pounds **Activity Level** Energetic **Shedding** Seasonal **Trainability** Eager to please **Life Expectancy** 12-15 years

If there ever was an overachiever in the canine kingdom, it would be the border collie. The breed is remarkably bright, athletic, easy to train, friendly, hardworking, agile, driven, and on and on. It was originally bred to herd sheep and has been called the world's greatest at the job because of its impressive method of stealth-crouching and explosive bursts of focused energy. Off the farm, the border collie is still a workaholic and is at its best when it feels functional—and that can be recreated through canine sports such as herding, agility or obedience trials, where the superstar breed can really show off its impressive talents.

Border Terrier
♛ Tough as Nails

AKC Breed Popularity No. 88
Temperament Gentle, independent, noble **Average Size** 12-15 inches, 11.5-15.5 pounds **Activity Level** Average **Shedding** Occasional **Trainability** Easy **Life Expectancy** 12-15 years

The border terrier might be small, but it is mighty. Bred to protect sheep from foxes, an animal twice its size, the little dog is tough as nails. Yet at home, it's happy and affectionate. The border terrier can adapt to the city, as long as it gets the proper amount of daily exercise (at least a brisk 30-minute walk on a leash, or a play session). The breed gets along well with kids and dogs—cats, on the other hand, will only stoke its hunting instincts.

DID YOU KNOW?
When Vikings invaded Britain, they crossed their spitzes with Roman dogs, creating the border collie.

Borzoi
♛ Most Glamorous

AKC Breed Popularity No.103
Temperament Affectionate, loyal, regally defined **Average Size**
26 inches and up, 60-105 pounds **Activity Level** Energetic **Shedding** Seasonal **Trainability** Independent **Life Expectancy** 9-14 years

A favorite of Russian aristocracy, the borzoi is one of the most physically impressive dogs. Its luxurious silky coat cloaks a greyhound-like body—and it shares that breed's speed. In full stride, the borzoi, which means "swift" in Russian, can reach 35 to 40 mph. Due to its size and athleticism, the sight hound requires daily exercise, be it long walks on a leash or running around a fenced-in yard. Just don't expect much roughhousing from this calm and dignified dog!

Boston Terrier
♛ Most Dapper

AKC Breed Popularity No. 88
Temperament Friendly, intelligent, amusing **Average Size** 15-17 inches, 12-25 pounds **Activity Level** Average **Shedding** Infrequent **Trainability** Eager to please **Life Expectancy** 11-13 years

With a "tuxedo" coat, it's no surprise the Boston terrier is nicknamed "The American Gentleman." But that also

Boxer

10th MOST POPULAR BREED!

Boykin Spaniel

describes its disposition: "dapper," "friendly" and "bright" are just a few adjectives that define this well-balanced dog. With a name like Boston terrier, of course, the breed is well suited for city life. Every dog's exercise needs are different, but for the most part, the Boston terrier needs only a brisk walk once or twice a day. So a jaunt to the local park or café while its owners get their morning caffeine fix should be enough—and it will allow the people-oriented dog to mingle.

Bouvier de Flandres
🏵 **Most Fearless**
AKC Breed Popularity No. 84
Temperament Affectionate, courageous, strong-willed **Average Size** 23.5-27.5 inches, 70-110 pounds
Activity Level Energetic **Shedding** Seasonal **Trainability** Agreeable
Life Expectancy 10-12 years

For such an exotic name, it might be surprising that the Bouvier de Flandres originally earned its keep doing just about everything on a farm: guarding and herding cattle, hauling product to market—even

Bouvier de Flandres

churning butter! The breed's burly and muscular body, accented by a beard and mustache, is as massive as its heart. And it's happiest when it has a job to do, just like in its early days in Belgium. For the modern Bouvier de Flandres, that can be serving as watchdog for its family, competing in canine sports or even assisting in search and rescue.

Boxer
🏵 **Most Well-Rounded**
AKC Breed Popularity No. 11
Temperament Fun, bright **Average Size** 21.5-25 inches, 50-80 pounds
Activity Level Energetic **Shedding** Occasional **Trainability** Easy
Life Expectancy 10-12 years

So named because it spars with its front paws, the boxer is powerful, graceful and fearless. These traits, plus its intelligence and work ethic, are why the breed is the go-to for countless jobs, from police dog to guide for the blind. The breed is so clever, in fact, that "it's important that the trainer be smarter than the dog," notes Stephanie Abraham of the American Boxers Club. Despite the boxer's intimidating stature, it's more of a lover than a fighter: Playful, affectionate, protective and sometimes silly, the dog with

boundless energy is an excellent playmate. "They just love kids," adds Abraham. "They are tolerant of even the naughtiest children. The boxer is truly the ultimate family dog"—and, ideally, should be the only canine in the household.

Boykin Spaniel
🏵 **Most Delightful**
AKC Breed Popularity No. 100
Temperament Friendly, eager, lovable **Average Size** 14-18 inches, 25-40 pounds **Activity Level** Average
Shedding Seasonal **Trainability** Eager to please **Life Expectancy** 10-15 years

Larger than the cocker spaniel yet more compact than the springer spaniel, the Boykin spaniel, the official dog of South Carolina, is considered the state's best-kept secret. Throughout the 20th century, the tenacious breed, which has webbed toes and can swim like a seal, was utilized to flush and retrieve waterfowl from lakes and swamps. In recent years, though, the rest of the country has caught on, unable to resist the Boykin's charms as a mellow, gentle, sweet and loyal family pet. Generally easy to train because of its high intellect, the breed is good with both kids and other dogs—the perfect companions for its playful spirit.

Briard

Brittany

Brussels
Griffon

Bull
Terrier

Briard

♔ Funniest Face

AKC Breed Popularity No. 132
Temperament Confident, smart,
faithful **Average Size** 22-27 inches,
55-100 pounds **Activity Level**
Average **Shedding** Infrequent
Trainability Independent **Life
Expectancy** 12 years

With its peekaboo hairdo and bushy
beard and eyebrows, it's impossible
not to look at the Briard and smile.
While its wavy coat does require a
bit of upkeep (it should be brushed
several times a week, with a good-
quality pin brush), the love and
loyalty it gives in return is well worth
the time spent on grooming. And
with its origins as a herder in France
dating back to the 1800s, the Briard's
natural instinct is to keep a protective
eye (under all that fur) on its human
flock, especially children.
It's also important to
remember that a dog
of this size needs
a fair amount of
exercise, whether
it's joining its owner
on a jog or bike ride
or simply playing fetch
in a fenced-in yard. The
Briard has a zest for life—and
its family must, too!

**DID YOU
KNOW?**
As minister to France,
Thomas Jefferson
fell in love with Briards
and brought one
back with him
to the U.S.

Brittany

♔ Most Versatile

AKC Breed Popularity No. 26
Temperament Bright, fun-loving,
upbeat **Average Size** 17.5-20.5
inches, 30-40 pounds **Activity
Level** Energetic **Shedding** Seasonal
Trainability Eager to please
Life Expectancy 12-14 years

As one of the world's most versatile
bird dogs, the Brittany possesses as
many skills as its prey has feathers.
Agile, athletic, bright, tireless and
enthusiastic, the breed (and its
excellent nose) is capable of working
on duck, pheasant, partridge,
woodcock and more. Its eagerness
is written all over its gorgeous
face—specifically, its high-set ears.
As expected with a sporting dog of
this capacity, the Brittany requires
a lot of exercise as well as activities
that stimulate its mind, like
obedience, agility, fly-ball
and dock-diving trials.
If the dog is utilized
as a hunting partner,
that's the most ideal.
Otherwise, an active
and adventurous
family is an equally
perfect fit, since that
combines two of the
Brittany's favorite things: its
companions and the outdoors.

Brussels Griffon

♔ Personality Plus

AKC Breed Popularity No. 98
Temperament Loyal, alert, curious
Average Size 7-10 inches, 8-10 pounds
Activity Level Average **Shedding**
Seasonal **Trainability** Agreeable
Life Expectancy 12-15 years

The Brussels griffon equals its
weight in personality! The amusing
dog is beloved for its complex
character and expressive face. The
breed also comes in a number of
varieties: a smooth or rough coat
and in one of four colors. Sociable
and devoted, the Brussels griffon
will closely bond to its humans,
following them from room to
room. It doesn't take much for
the sensitive breed to feel lonely;
if left by itself for long periods
of time, the dog will exhibit
undesirable behaviors to express
its frustration. Although playful, it
is toy-size and not recommended
for kids who like to roughhouse.

Bull Terrier

♔ Most Unique Head

AKC Breed Popularity No. 62
Temperament Playful, charming,
mischievous **Average Size** 21-22
inches, 50-70 pounds **Activity
Level** Energetic **Shedding** Seasonal
Trainability Independent
Life Expectancy 12-13 years

The Bull Terrier's personality is
as unique as its "egg head." One
of the most comical breeds, it's

a freethinker that loves to enjoy life with its owner. The dog can be stubborn and challenging to train, but if handled firmly yet positively—and with lots of patience, humor and treats—it can excel at everything from canine sports to assisting in bomb detection. Those interested in the breed should be aware: It needs a diet that includes natural calcium, especially as a growing puppy.

Bulldog

5th
MOST POPULAR BREED!

Bullmastiff

C

Bulldog
🏅 **Biggest Lap Dog**
AKC Breed Popularity No. 5
Temperament Friendly, courageous, calm **Average Size** 14-15 inches, 40-50 pounds **Activity Level** Average **Shedding** Regular **Trainability** Agreeable **Life Expectancy** 8-10 years

There's no mistaking a bulldog: muscular, low-slung body; massive head, with a pushed-in nose; hanging chops; and, of course, an undershot jaw. But its distinctive look also requires extra care. The breed's short muzzle can make breathing difficult in heat and humidity, and owners need to be vigilant that the dog doesn't become overheated. The wrinkles on the bulldog's face also need to be checked regularly to make sure the skin is kept clean and dry (a cotton ball dipped in peroxide, followed by cornstarch to absorb the moisture, should do the trick). In return, the bulldog is an easygoing, sweet and friendly companion who loves its family so much, it'll want to curl up

in your lap—regardless of the fact that it weighs up to 50 pounds.

Bullmastiff
🏅 **Most Protective**
AKC Breed Popularity No. 51
Temperament Affectionate, loyal, brave **Average Size** 24-27 inches, 100-130 pounds **Activity Level** Energetic **Shedding** Seasonal **Trainability** Agreeable **Life Expectancy** 7-9 years

A cross between the bulldog and the mastiff, two of the most powerful breeds, the combination resulted in a world-class family protector with a heart as big as its build. While energetic, the bullmastiff is not exactly active; moderate exercise, such as a brisk walk, will do just fine. Any activity should not happen immediately before or after the dog has eaten, to avoid the risk of bloat—a condition in which the stomach distends and twists. Puppies should be enrolled in obedience classes while they're small enough to control and there should be rules in place for the dog as it grows up.

Cairn Terrier
🏅 **Best Little Pal**
AKC Breed Popularity No. 69
Temperament Alert, cheerful
Average Size 10 inches, 14 pounds
Activity Level Average **Shedding** Occasional **Trainability** Agreeable
Life Expectancy 13-15 years

Small yet sturdy, the cairn terrier will sit on your lap and then frolic in the yard. Originally bred to dig into cairns, or mounds of stones, in order to chase out rodents, it has maintained that instinct—so it's important to give the curious dog space to explore. Obedience training will help curb its impulse to chase after small animals, but owners should be aware that it will always remain and take proper precautions, like always keeping the dog on a leash in unsecured areas. Ever adaptable, the cairn is just as much at home in the city as it is the country—so long as it gets daily exercise.

Cairn Terrier

Canaan Dog

Canaan Dog
♘ Most Self-Reliant

AKC Breed Popularity No. 179
Temperament Confident, alert, vigilant **Average Size** 19-24 inches, 35-55 pounds **Activity Level** Average **Shedding** Frequent **Trainability** Independent **Life Expectancy** 12-15 years

One of the oldest breeds, the Canaan dog of today has retained many of its instincts from 2,000 years of fending for itself in the deserts of Israel. Self-possessed and aloof with strangers, with its family it's always on guard as their fierce protector (evidenced by its erect ears). Early training is key for the clever breed, as it can tend to make itself pack leader of the home, unless its owners establish themselves when the dog is young. Highly intelligent and easily trainable, the Canaan dog makes an affectionate and devoted family member that will simply adore its human companions.

Cane Corso
♘ Best Bodyguard

AKC Breed Popularity No. 32
Temperament Affectionate, intelligent, majestic **Average Size** 23.5-27.5 inches, 88-110 pounds

Activity Level Energetic **Shedding** Occasional **Trainability** Agreeable **Life Expectancy** 9-12 years

Although there are scores of breeds that are known for their devotion to protection, none come close to the cane corso. In fact, the ancient Italian dog's name roughly translates to "bodyguard dog." With its massive head and body, the breed looks intimidating. But underneath that tough exterior is a softie that loves its family—but only after proper training as a puppy. Between its dominant nature and size, owners can easily find themselves in a subordinate position, with the dog as the boss of the household. Just as important as training is daily exercise: A brisk 1-mile walk or run, twice a day, is ideal to maintain its mental and physical health.

DID YOU KNOW?
The Cardigan Welsh corgi is built low to the ground so it doesn't get kicked by cattle while herding.

Cane Corso

Cardigan Welsh Corgi
♘ Social Butterfly

AKC Breed Popularity No. 68
Temperament Affectionate, loyal, smart **Average Size** 10.5-12.5 inches, 25-38 pounds **Activity Level** Energetic **Shedding** Seasonal **Trainability** Agreeable **Life Expectancy** 12-15 years

Very similar to the more popular Pembroke Welsh corgi, the quickest way to distinguish the Cardigan Welsh corgi is a look at its tail: It has one, while its younger cousin does not. The sweet-faced breed is also incredibly sociable. It adores not only its family (including small children and other dogs) but also anyone it encounters on its daily outings. The Cardigan Welsh corgi is especially noted for its adaptability, to both surroundings and interests. Basically, whatever its human companion wants to do—whether that's enjoying a fun physical activity or simply sitting on the couch, binge-watching a TV series—the dog is down for it...although if asked, it would certainly suggest a game of fetch in the yard.

Cardigan Welsh Corgi

Cavalier King Charles Spaniel

⚜ Most Adaptable

AKC Breed Popularity No. 18 **Temperament** Independent, smart, poised **Average Size** 12-13 inches, 13-18 pounds **Activity Level** Calm **Shedding** Occasional **Trainability** Eager to please **Life Expectancy** 12-15 years

What else would you expect from a breed named after a king of England? The Cavalier King Charles spaniel has been a favorite of British monarchs for centuries, and today it remains one of the most popular pups in the world. Beloved for its sweet face, silky coat (which comes in four distinct color patterns), intellect, grace and even temper, the Cavalier King Charles is simply delightful and undemanding. Whether its owner wants to go on a walk or relax at home, the dog is always a willing participant. The friendly breed, which is easy to train, also does well with children and other pets and makes a fantastic therapy dog.

Cesky Terrier

⚜ Best-Kept Secret

AKC Breed Popularity No. 185 **Temperament** Clever, adventurous, family-oriented **Average Size** 10-13 inches, 14-24 pounds **Activity Level** Average **Shedding** Occasional **Trainability** Agreeable **Life Expectancy** 12-15 years

Although not one of the most popular breeds, the Cesky terrier is an all-around quality family pet. Mellow, protective and bright, the Czechoslovakian dog is also rather scarce: Only about 600 are recorded to be living in the U.S. Those lucky enough to open their home to a Cesky are in for a special treat, because the versatile terrier can be everything from an adventurous playmate for children to a calm companion for an older owner. It's also an instinctual hunter, and its high prey drive should be managed early on with obedience training.

18th MOST POPULAR BREED!

Cavalier King Charles Spaniel

Cesky Terrier

Best Breeds for Apartments

The bigger the dog, the more space they require? Not exactly. Apartment dwellers are not limited to teacup pups. There's a fair number of midsize and larger breeds who also do just fine in smaller homes.

BOSTON TERRIER
Not only does the breed require a moderate amount of exercise, they are also relatively easy to train. Live in a high-rise and don't want to make the trek up and down for late-night potty breaks? A training pad will do the trick!

CAVALIER KING CHARLES SPANIEL
Their moderate energy is a win on many levels: A quiet demeanor means that there's less noise to annoy the neighbors, and just one walk a day is needed!

FRENCH BULLDOG
Minimal exercise plus maximum snuggling is the name of the Frenchie's game. And as with the Boston, training pads can be a wise investment, if you don't live on the ground floor.

GREYHOUND
Although known for their speed, it's a misconception that greyhounds need a yard to run around in: They're actually big couch potatoes. Still, be prepared to take them on a long walk or to a local dog run to burn off energy.

ITALIAN GREYHOUND
Just like greyhounds, their toy counterparts love nothing more than to curl up next to their loved ones as they watch TV or read a good book (after a nice long walk, of course). Greyhounds and IGs also tend to not be big barkers.

POMERANIAN
City life suits Poms just fine—and not only because they don't need a lot of space to run and play. The breed's temperament allows for them to be easily transported in a dog carrier.

YORKSHIRE TERRIER
When it comes to this breed, big things really do come in small packages. While the Yorkie is relatively tiny, its personality makes up for the lack of size. Plus they don't require much exercise, which is perfect for life in a smaller home.

Chinese Crested

Chihuahua

Chesapeake Bay Retriever

Chinese Shar-Pei

Chinook

Chesapeake Bay Retriever
Best Swimmer

AKC Breed Popularity No. 45
Temperament Affectionate, bright, sensitive **Average Size** 21-26 inches, 55-80 pounds **Activity Level** Energetic **Shedding** Regular **Trainability** Agreeable **Life Expectancy** 10-13 years

Originally bred in the 19th century to be a duck dog in the Mid-Atlantic region for which it's named, the Chesapeake Bay retriever is a magnificent and impressive creature: A waterproof coat, webbed feet, keen sense of smell, tireless stamina and indefatigable athleticism, along with its dashing good looks, put it in a class all its own. Its personality traits are also highly desirable. As a family pet, the Chessie, as its called, is affectionate and loyal—and with an ambivalence toward strangers, it makes for an excellent watchdog. The breed is also sensitive and serves as a perceptive therapy dog. For Chessies who are especially active to high-energy, a diet with at least 20 percent protein is advised, to fuel its abilities.

Chihuahua
Most Sassy

AKC Breed Popularity No. 33
Temperament Charming, graceful, saucy **Average Size** 5-8 inches, not exceeding 6 pounds **Activity Level** Average **Shedding** Occasional **Trainability** Independent **Life Expectancy** 14-16 years

For such a tiny dog, the Chihuahua has one of the biggest personalities. Notorious for trying to rule its household with a confident big-dog attitude (and manipulative cuteness), the clever breed must receive obedience training early to establish its owner as the boss. Although adaptable enough to live in the bustling city or tranquil country, the Chihuahua, which typically doesn't exceed 6 pounds, should be properly dressed to protect it from cold weather. Similarly, the teacup pup is too small to roughhouse with children—yet a cozy lap will do just fine.

Chinese Crested
Coolest Hairdo

AKC Breed Popularity No. 797
Temperament Affectionate, alert, lively **Average Size** 11-13 inches, 8-12 pounds **Activity Level** Average **Shedding** Infrequent **Trainability** Agreeable **Life Expectancy** 13-18 years

The Chinese crested's personality is as fun as its unique look. The breed recognized for its spiky hairdo and soft-skinned body is frisky, loving, elegant, attentive and devoted to its human companion. While being hairless makes the Chinese crested odor-free and keeps shedding to a bare minimum, it also creates its own set of necessary special care. Because the dog's skin is exposed, it's prone to irritations, allergies and especially sunburn. When the breed is outside for daily walks or romps in the yard, sunscreen should be applied (protective clothing will also do the trick).

Chinese Shar-Pei
Most Wrinkly

AKC Breed Popularity No. 64
Temperament Loyal, independent, calm **Average Size** 18-20 inches, 45-60 pounds **Activity Level** Average **Shedding** Regular **Trainability** May be stubborn **Life Expectancy** 8-12 years

The Chinese shar-pei is a one-of-a-kind dog... and not just physically. Adored for its wrinkly, sandpapery coat (shar-pei translates to "sand skin"), the breed is endlessly loyal, smart, regal and serene. But it's also rather stubborn, which can be challenging unless managed with early obedience training and socialization. If not, the dominant dog will think it's the leader of the pack and do as it pleases. Another task that should be introduced at a young age: weekly ear cleanings. But don't use cotton swabs or hydrogen peroxide; instead, "float" any debris out of the canal using an ear-cleaning solution.

Chow Chow

Cirneco dell'Etna

Chinook
🏅 Worst Watch Dog
AKC Breed Popularity No. 190 **Temperament** Smart, patient, devoted **Average Size** 22-26 inches, 50-90 pounds **Activity Level** Average **Shedding** Seasonal **Trainability** Eager to please **Life Expectancy** 12-15 years

Although most of the world might not be familiar with the incredibly scarce Chinook, it's the pride of its home state, New Hampshire. The outgoing breed is remarkably people-oriented (with a special feel for children)—but, perhaps, to a fault. Friendly and affectionate, the Chinook would fail as a fierce guard dog, no matter how much training it received. Still, it should be taught not to jump all over its beloved humans to express affection. If properly trained, the Chinook can be reliable off-leash for outdoor activities, such as walks, hikes, bicycle rides, camping trips, even boating adventures.

Chow Chow
🏅 Most Clean
AKC Breed Popularity No. 75 **Temperament** Dignified, bright, serious-minded **Average Size** 17-20 inches, 45-70 pounds **Activity Level** Average **Shedding** Seasonal **Trainability** May be stubborn **Life Expectancy** 8-12 years

One of the oldest breeds, dating back to circa 200 B.C., the chow chow is a timeless delight. Its lion's mane aside, the dog is intelligent, loyal and serene—and also incredibly clean. Not only does the chow chow have very little odor, but it housebreaks easily and is almost catlike in its meticulous self-bathing with its tongue. It needs only moderate exercise, like a leisurely walk a few times a day, but should avoid outdoor activity during hot periods—chows don't tolerate heat or humidity well.

Cirneco dell'Etna
🏅 Most Durable
AKC Breed Popularity No. 183 **Temperament** Affectionate, friendly, independent **Average Size** 16.5-19.5 inches, 17-26 pounds **Activity Level** Energetic **Shedding** Infrequent **Trainability** Independent **Life Expectancy** 12-14 years

Despite its primitive origins, the Cirneco dell'Etna is a remarkably gentle and loyal family pet. Bred to be an independent hunter of rabbit and game, the dog was quite durable and able to go without food or water for hours in ancient Sicily's hot climate. According to legend, 1,000 Cirnechi dell'Etna even guarded a temple located on the slopes of Mount Etna, Europe's largest active volcano. These days, the intelligent and inquisitive dog is content to be an interactive family member, enjoying long walks and activities with its humans. Although slightly more trainable than the typical sight hound, the breed does have a strong prey drive and should never be allowed off-leash in an unsecured area. Similarly, caution is advised when introducing the dog to cats or other small animals.

Clumber Spaniel
♀ Biggest Drooler
AKC Breed Popularity No. 143
Temperament Mellow, amusing, gentlemanly **Average Size** 17-20 inches, 55-85 pounds **Activity Level** Average **Shedding** Regular **Trainability** Agreeable
Life Expectancy 10-12 years

For a powerful breed developed to hunt birds, the Clumber spaniel is considerably sedate—as long as it's not working. Inside the home, the dog is easygoing and sweet and enjoys curling up on the couch. Although wary of strangers, it's not much of a barker, so don't expect a vigilant watchdog. The breed does have a mischievous side, making it a fun playmate for children. The Clumber spaniel's only shortcoming: It drools quite a bit—but it will look cute doing it.

Cocker Spaniel
♀ Silkiest Coat
AKC Breed Popularity No. 30
Temperament Gentle, smart, happy **Average Size** 13.5-15.5 inches, 20-30 pounds **Activity Level** Average **Shedding** Occasional **Trainability** Eager to please
Life Expectancy 10-14 years

Cocker Spaniel

Clumber Spaniel

Collie

Coton de Tulear

One of the most popular American breeds, the cocker spaniel is a playful dog with dreamy eyes and a mischievous personality. Although developed to hunt woodcock (hence "cocker"), the breed has become an in-demand family pet: It's a medium size dog that is great with kids, athletic, easy to train and, above all, a very merry companion. The cocker spaniel is also a stunning sight to behold, with its lush coat and feathered ears. But it's not exactly wash-and-wear: Regular grooming sessions are required and should include daily comb-throughs to remove loose hair, thorough bathing with a quality dog shampoo (rinsed and re-rinsed, since soap residue can cause irritation), topped off with a blow-dry. Or it might be easier to find a professional groomer.

Collie
♀ Sweetest Disposition
AKC Breed Popularity No. 387
Temperament Trustworthy, steadfast, industrious **Average Size** 22-26 inches, 50-75 pounds **Activity Level** Average **Shedding** Seasonal **Trainability** Easy **Life Expectancy** 12-14 years
One of the world's most recognized breeds (thanks to Lassie), the collie is a majestic animal, with its showy coat (which can be rough or smooth) and first-rate character. So many qualities make the breed an ideal family pet, especially its famous love of children and loyalty to family. The collie thrives on human companionship. It's also keenly intelligent and enjoys learning, which makes obedience training relatively easy. But with such an athletic dog, why stop there? Agility, herding and lure-coursing are all canine sports the collie can excel at with impressive talent.

Coton de Tulear
♀ Biggest Charmer
AKC Breed Popularity No. 81
Temperament Charming, bright, happy-go-lucky **Average Size** 9-11 inches, 8-15 pounds **Activity Level** Average **Shedding** Occasional **Trainability** Easy **Life Expectancy** 15-19 years

While some breeds were developed to hunt, others, like the coton de Tulear, are purely for companionship—a job it excels at naturally. The little white dog who feels soft as cotton (hence its name) is the epitome of charm: It loves nothing more than to amuse and comfort its beloved humans. With a coat so white and profuse, it does require a bit of grooming. Unless the dog is given a short "puppy cut," it will need daily brushing—and don't forget spray conditioner, to avoid breakage! What else would you expect from the Royal Dog of Madagascar?

Curly-Coated Retriever
🏵 **Great Swimmer**
AKC Breed Popularity No. 162
Temperament Confident, proud, wickedly smart **Average Size** 23–27 inches, 60–95 pounds **Activity Level** Energetic **Shedding** Occasional **Trainability** Independent
Life Expectancy 10-12 years

It may look more suited for a beauty pageant than the hunting field, but the curly-coated retriever is truly a versatile and tireless gun dog. Its distinctive coat is more than just lovely to look at: The tight curls are waterproof and thorn-resistant. And surprisingly, it's very wash-and-wear. The curly-coated retriever doesn't need to be brushed, because its coat will frizz, like some human hair. Instead, an infrequent wet-down and air-dry will do. The breed, with its independent personality, is just as effortless: It loves to play and

Curly-Coated Retriever

cuddle its owners and is recognized for its "good manners" (as a result of obedience training).

12th MOST POPULAR BREED!

Dachshund

Dachshund
🏵 **Most Distinctive Body**
AKC Breed Popularity No. 12
Temperament Friendly, curious, spunky **Average Size** 8-9 inches, 16-32 pounds (standard); 5-6 inches, 11 pounds and under (miniature)
Activity Level Average **Shedding** Occasional **Trainability** Agreeable
Life Expectancy 12-16 years

The dachshund comes in two sizes (miniature and standard) and one of three coat types (smooth, wirehaired or longhaired)—but all share its famously defining physical trait, a long body and short legs. And the breed's personality is just endearing: animated, intelligent, social and brave. It's a little dog with a big-dog bark who will act as protector of its family. And it doesn't ask for much

in return, other than that its owner keep careful vigilance so the dog doesn't run up and down stairs or jump off furniture, which can injure its back. Dachshunds shed moderately, have very little odor and don't require much grooming, regardless of coat: Smooth is relatively wash-and-wear; long-haired may need frequent brushing; wirehaired can be plucked several times a year, with beard trimmings in between.

Dalmatian

Dalmatian
🏵 **Best Spots**
AKC Breed Popularity No. 56
Temperament Dignified, smart, outgoing **Average Size** 19-24 inches, 45-70 pounds **Activity Level** Energetic **Shedding** Frequent **Trainability** Agreeable
Life Expectancy 11-13 years

Although the Dalmatian is associated with firehouses, it's been a working dog since as far back as the 1800s, when it accompanied horse-drawn carriages. And that instinct to protect remains today— it's a loyal and intelligent watchdog who is standoffish with strangers. But also because of its origins, the breed is high-energy and requires regular exercise to burn it off, whether by playing fetch in the yard, going on a long hike or running alongside its owner during a jog or bike ride.

Dandie Dinmont Terrier
⚜ Rough and Tumble

AKC Breed Popularity No. 176
Temperament Independent, smart, proud **Average Size** 8-11 inches, 18-24 pounds **Activity Level** Average **Shedding** Infrequent **Trainability** Independent **Life Expectancy** 12-15 years

Don't be fooled by the Dandie Dinmont terrier's name, dainty appearance or royal lineage as a pampered pooch of 19th-century French king Louis Philippe: The breed is a sturdy little dog with a big personality and tough-guy mind-set. It will act as a devoted watchdog—and has the deep bark to back it up. Originally bred for the rigors of farm life, the Dandie Dinmont is quite adaptable and can be at ease living in the city. It also does well with children and enjoys playing with them; just be sure it's always in a properly secured area. Since its instinct is to hunt, the dog, no matter how well-trained, will dart off if it spots prey.

Doberman Pinscher
⚜ Great Watchdog

AKC Breed Popularity No. 17
Temperament Loyal, fearless, alert **Average Size** 24-28 inches, 60-100 pounds **Activity Level** Energetic **Shedding** Regularly **Trainability** Eager to please **Life Expectancy** 10-12 years

The intimidating yet sleek breed is a leading watchdog—and also a trusted companion, since "they bond so closely to us," says Doberman Pinscher Club of America's Shani St. John. "They are full of heart." Given the dog's power, it does require a lot of exercise. "It's easy for dogs to be well-behaved when their bodies are active and minds properly stimulated," adds St. John, who says Dobermans can also be great with little ones—"but they need a family that understands how children should interact with dogs."

Dogue de Bordeaux
⚜ Gentle Giant

AKC Breed Popularity No. 67
Temperament Affectionate, loyal, courageous **Average Size** 23-27 inches, 99 pounds and up **Activity Level**

Average **Shedding** Regular **Trainability** Agreeable **Life Expectancy** 5-8 years

The French breed is so ancient, it's been around since Julius Caesar conquered the region in the first century B.C. and turned the dogue de Bordeaux into a Roman gladiator. It has a massive head and strapping body, but looks can be deceiving. While certainly protective, the DDB is also incredibly sweet and would prefer showering its owner in slobbery kisses. It's also sensitive, something to keep in mind during training: While firmness is necessary, harsh discipline will do more harm than good.

Dutch Shepherd
⚜ Most Intuitive

AKC Breed Popularity N/A
Temperament Intelligent, lively, athletic **Average Size** 21.5-24.5 inches, 42-75 pounds **Activity Level** Energetic **Shedding** Seasonal **Trainability** Agreeable **Life Expectancy** 11-14 years

One of the breeds that most closely resembles a wolf, the Dutch shepherd is smart, alert and athletic and makes an excellent canine companion—all reasons that it's often utilized as a K-9 for police and military work. It's also incredibly devoted to its human, and whether that's a single person or bustling family, the Dutch shepherd knows how to adjust its energy and demeanor accordingly.

17th MOST POPULAR BREED!

Dandie Dinmont Terrier

Doberman Pinscher

Dogue de Bordeaux

Dutch Shepherd

English Cocker Spaniel

English Cocker Spaniel
🏅 **Happy-Go-Lucky**
AKC Breed Popularity No. 52
Temperament Energetic, merry, responsive **Average Size** 15-17 inches, 26-34 pounds **Activity Level** Average **Shedding** Occasional **Trainability** Eager to please **Life Expectancy** 12-14 years

A common misconception about the English cocker spaniel is that it's merely a variety of cocker spaniel when, in actuality, it's a separate breed (and remarkably well-balanced). And it is cherished for its merry disposition, devotion and agreeableness. According to owners, whether the bird dog is working in the field or at home lounging on the sofa, its tail rarely stops wagging. Like any active sporting dog, the English cocker spaniel requires daily exercise—and always on a leash or in a fenced-in yard, because of its instinct to hunt. And while its silky coat is gorgeous, the hair is profuse and demands regular care, including a thorough weekly brushing to prevent tangles and maintain its neat appearance.

English Foxhound
🏅 **Most Primal**
AKC Breed Popularity No. 188
Temperament Affectionate, gentle, sociable **Average Size** 24 inches, 60-75 pounds **Activity Level Energetic Shedding** Regular **Trainability** Agreeable **Life Expectancy** 10-13 years

Slightly more popular than its American counterpart, the English foxhound is the epitome of beauty and practicality. The scent-driven hound, while gentle and loving, is so primal that it's rarely seen as a pet (and best left to experienced huntsmen), unless the home is occupied by multiple people and dogs so that it feels it's part of a pack. Similarly, the English foxhound is not suitable for apartment living, as it requires plenty of space, ideally a large fenced-in yard, to burn off its high energy. Yet once inside, the dog is relaxed and happy to curl up and relax with its companion.

English Setter
🏅 **Biggest Sweetheart**
AKC Breed Popularity No. 94
Temperament Friendly, mellow, merry **Average Size** 23-27 inches, 45-80 pounds **Activity Level** Energetic **Shedding** Regular **Trainability** Easy **Life Expectancy** 12 years

English Foxhound

The disposition of the English setter is as beautiful as its unique, speckled coat. Although bred to hunt, the dog is just as devoted to being a companion and is quite sweet and good-natured with other dogs and people. Because of its strong prey drive, proper training is vital from a young age, as an English setter puppy is especially curious about everything in its world. Even into adulthood, the breed is incredibly food-driven and known to "counter surf" (and, in extreme cases, get into the dishwasher!) if its nose picks up on something that smells yummy.

English Setter

English Spring Spaniel
♦ Most Soulful Eyes

AKC Breed Popularity No. 27
Temperament Friendly, playful, obedient **Average Size** 19-20 inches, 40-50 pounds **Activity Level** Average **Shedding** Occasional **Trainability** Eager to please **Life Expectancy** 12-14 years

The English springer spaniel is a bird dog cherished for its dual personalty: well-mannered companion at home, trusted hunting buddy in the field. And because it was bred to work so closely with humans (its job is to "spring" birds from cover), it's highly trainable and eager to please. The dog also craves company and is thrilled to be included in any family activity, although fetching and swimming are preferred pastimes. Despite its great energy, with regular exercise the breed can be suitable to live in an apartment or small house.

English Springer Spaniel

English Toy Spaniel

DID YOU KNOW?
Mary, Queen of Scots' favorite English toy spaniel refused to leave her side, even at her execution.

Field Spaniel

English Toy Spaniel
♦ People-Pleaser

AKC Breed Popularity No. 135
Temperament Gentle, playful, intelligent **Average Size** 9-10 inches, 8-14 pounds **Activity Level** Regular exercise **Shedding** Seasonal **Trainability** Independent **Life Expectancy** 10-12 years

Bred to be a companion for royals, the English toy spaniel has been a pampered lap dog for centuries—and has the personality to prove it: proud (yet affectionate) with owners and discriminating with outsiders. The breed needs only moderate exercise, making it a perfect choice for apartment dwellers. Be careful not to keep the dog outdoors too long in hot or humid weather, since it's short-faced. Maintain the toy spaniel's beauty by brushing its silky coat twice a week and washing it with a gentle shampoo every four to six weeks.

Entlebucher Mountain Dog
♦ Bundle of Energy

AKC Breed Popularity No. 157
Temperament Loyal, smart, enthusiastic **Average Size** 16-21 inches, 40-65 pounds **Activity Level** Energetic **Shedding** Infrequent **Trainability** Independent **Life Expectancy** 11-13 years

Bred to herd cattle, the Entlebucher mountain dog is naturally equipped with the strength to move an animal more than 20 times its size. But that energy can sometimes seem boundless, and if the dog isn't working, at least an hour of exercise a day is necessary to channel it, making the breed ideal mostly for active people who enjoy running or biking. The Entlebucher instinctively is happiest when it has a job: At home, that can be as the devoted protector of its two-legged (and also, four-legged) "herd" or as a durable playmate for older children. On the field, the clever and athletic dog would excel as a participant in just about any canine sport, especially obedience, tracking, agility and herding.

Entlebucher Mountain Dog

Finnish Lapphund

Finnish Spitz

Field Spaniel
♜ Major Foodie

AKC Breed Popularity No. 149
Temperament Sweet, fun-loving, sensitive **Average Size** 17-18 inches, 35-50 pounds **Activity Level** Average **Shedding** Regularly **Trainability** Agreeable **Life Expectancy** 12-13 years

Although not as popular as its cousins, the cocker spaniel and the springer spaniel, the field spaniel sits in a class all its own. It has a winning combination of beauty, charm and practicality. Despite the breed's energetic spirit, which requires regular physical and mental activity, it's surprisingly docile and loves downtime with its family, making the field spaniel a trustworthy companion for kids. A "thinking dog," the breed is easily trainable—and because it's incredibly food-driven, it also doesn't need much motivation beyond a yummy treat (and a "good dog" from its owner).

Finnish Lapphund
♜ Most Compassionate

AKC Breed Popularity No. 161
Temperament Friendly, alert, agile **Average Size** 16-21 inches, 33-53 pounds **Activity Level** Average **Shedding** Seasonal **Trainability** Eager to please **Life Expectancy** 12-15 years

Originally bred to herd reindeer in the Arctic Circle, the Finnish Lapphund isn't just an ideal dog for Santa Claus. Beloved for being one of the friendliest breeds, it craves companionship and especially enjoys being part of the family, which it considers its pack. Despite its double coat, the Finnish Lapphund needs only minimal grooming and doesn't typically have a doggie odor. The breed is known to be quick learners and likely to excel at canine sports that allow pups to show off their obedience and agility.

Finnish Spitz
♜ Fearless Hunter

AKC Breed Popularity No. 184
Temperament Friendly, good-natured, lively **Average Size** 15.5-20 inches, 20-33 pounds **Activity Level** Energetic **Shedding** Seasonal **Trainability** Agreeable **Life Expectancy** 13-15 years

With its flame-colored fur and ability to yodel, the Finnish spitz is a bold dog that happens to look just like a fox. And it's not for the inactive: Bred to hunt all day, Finns have strong stamina, which requires a high degree of exercise; Just be sure it's always on-leash or in a fenced-in yard. The breed is also capable of excelling at canine sports, though training could prove challenging: Finns are so incredibly smart, the dog can easily get bored if sessions aren't kept short and sweet.

Flat-Coated Retriever
♜ Eternal Optimist

AKC Breed Popularity No. 89
Temperament Cheerful, optimistic **Average Size** 22-24.5 inches, 60-70 pounds **Activity Level** Energetic **Shedding** Regular **Trainability** Eager to please **Life Expectancy** 8-10 years

As one of the AKC's six retrievers (dogs trained to hunt downed waterfowl), the flat-coated retriever stands out among the pack. Known as the Peter Pan of the sporting group, it refuses to grow up and often retains its energetic puppy traits well into later years—which may not appeal to everyone. A good way to burn off that extra energy is long daily walks, play sessions or even agility activities. Since the breed is so eager to please its owner, training tends to be fairly easy.

Flat-Coated Retriever

French Bulldog
⚜ Biggest Personality

AKC Breed Popularity No. 4
Temperament Adaptable, playful, smart **Average Size** 11-13 inches, under 28 pounds **Activity Level** Calm **Shedding** Regular **Trainability** Agreeable **Life Expectancy** 10-12 years

The French bulldog may be small in size, but it certainly makes up for it in personality. The charming and affectionate pup is a wonderful companion and great for novice owners, since it doesn't require much fuss. Because its coat is short, very minimal grooming is needed—and the same goes for outdoor activity. "They don't need a lot of exercise," notes Virginia Rowland, a breeder and AKC judge of French bulldogs, "so they are good apartment dogs. A big backyard is wonderful for any dog, but not necessary for a French bulldog." The breed also gets along with just about everyone and easily adapts to owners, whether they're single, married or a family—but it does require bonding with its human(s). "Like most dogs, Frenchies love spending time with their families," adds Rowland. "If your work or other obligations means you are not home much, a Frenchie is probably not for you."

German Pinscher
⚜ Little Genius

AKC Breed Popularity No. 134
Temperament Courageous, intelligent, vivacious **Average Size** 17-20 inches, 25-45 pounds **Activity Level** Energetic **Shedding** Occasional **Trainability** Agreeable **Life Expectancy** 12-14 years

Considered the prototype of pinschers, it was originally bred to kill rats. These days, the alert and inquisitive German pinscher is content to work as its family's vigilant protector and companion. It's also incredibly intelligent—to the point where the dog can manipulate its owner, especially one who's a novice with canines. The German pinscher's high energy will need to be channeled into lots of daily exercise, but since it excels at a challenge (and performing), get the dog involved in canine sports, such as agility, tracking or barn hunts.

German Shepherd Dog

German Pinscher

DID YOU KNOW?
German shepherds gained popularity in the U.S. in the early 1900s, thanks to film star Rin Tin Tin.

2nd MOST POPULAR BREED!

German Shepherd Dog
⚜ Most Multifaceted

AKC Breed Popularity No. 2
Temperament Confident, courageous, smart **Average Size** 22-26 inches, 50-90 pounds **Activity Level** Average **Shedding** Regular **Trainability** Eager to please **Life Expectancy** 7-10 years

There's a good reason the German shepherd dog is the top choice for police and military forces: It's one of the finest in the species, noted for its character, intelligence, courage and loyalty. In the home, the GSD is a gentle pet and extremely devoted to its family. "They're your best buddy," describes Gary Szymczak, president of the German Shepherd Dog Club of America. As a large dog, the GSD requires regular exercise, but nothing out of the ordinary. Even just a brisk walk a few times a day will do. Because of the GSD's extraordinary brainpower, it's easy to train. "Once they learn something, they don't forget it," adds Szymczak. "The one thing about a shepherd is, they love to please. They know when you're happy. In my opinion, they're the perfect animal."

German Shorthaired Pointer
🏅 **Boundless Energy**

AKC Breed Popularity No.9
Temperament Friendly, smart, willing to please **Average Size** 21-25 inches, 45-75 pounds **Activity Level** Energetic **Shedding** Regular **Trainability** Eager to please **Life Expectancy** 10-12 years

The ultimate hunting dog, the German shorthaired pointer has power, agility, speed and endurance. Off the field, it needs vigorous exercise. "Two 30-minute walks a day won't do it," explains Patte Titus, head of education with the German Shorthaired Pointer Club of America. Outdoor activities, like running, hiking or throwing a ball, are necessary to burn off its boundless energy. Another essential for the intelligent GSP is training, starting as a puppy. Don't be discouraged if the dog needs extra effort as an adult: Females can be challenging until 3 years old; males, up to 5. "Think of teens with their first set of car keys on a Saturday night," describes Titus. "The breed is 'young at heart' and will continue to be active well into 10 to 12 years of age."

German Wirehaired Pointer
🏅 **Most Resilient**

AKC Breed Popularity No. 63
Temperament Affectionate, eager, enthusiastic **Average Size** 22-26 inches, 50-70 pounds **Activity Level** Energetic **Shedding** Regularly **Trainability** Eager to please **Life Expectancy** 14-16 years

Though similar to the popular GSP, the German wirehaired pointer is its own distinct breed, not just one with a different coat. The resilient dog is an all-weather, all-terrain hunter and more intense when it's working. But at home, the affectionate GWP is just as content to relax. It craves human companionship and makes quite an amusing family member, yet will get lonely and potentially destructive if left for long periods. Also, just like the GSP, the wirehaired is a high-energy dog and needs an outlet for it, whether that's long walks, play sessions or canine sports.

Giant Schnauzer
🏅 **Instinctive Protector**

AKC Breed Popularity No. 78
Temperament Loyal, alert, trainable **Average Size** 23.5-27.5 inches, 55-85 pounds **Activity Level** Energetic **Shedding** Infrequent **Trainability** Easy **Life Expectancy** 12-15 years

The biggest of the schnauzers, the giant was bred up from the standard in the mid-1800s to drive cattle and guard the farm. These days, the territorial dog's instinct is to protect the family it so dearly loves. And with its keen intelligence and alertness, it can quickly distinguish between friend and foe. Unlike other big breeds, the giant schnauzer is energetic and needs lots of exercise, making it an ideal buddy for someone who enjoys jogging, hiking or swimming. For those who aren't as active, long walks, play sessions with other dogs or a long game of fetch will suffice.

Glen of Imaal Terrier
🏅 **Most Laid-Back**

AKC Breed Popularity No. 174
Temperament Gentle, spirited, bold **Average Size** 12.5-14 inches, 32-40 pounds **Activity Level** Average **Shedding** Occasional **Trainability** Independent **Life Expectancy** 10-15 years

It may not be obvious from its adorable face and petite body, but the Glen of Imaal terrier was bred for hard work in the rocky Irish region after which it's named. Despite that, the docile dog has slightly curved front legs and shouldn't engage in more than moderate exercise, like short walks or chasing a ball around the house. While it will easily fall in love with humans, it's not a big fan of other dogs and should be the only pup in the home.

German Wirehaired Pointer

Giant Schnauzer

9th MOST POPULAR BREED!

German Shorthaired Pointer

Glen of Imaal Terrier

3rd MOST POPULAR BREED!

Golden Retriever

Golden Retriever
Sweetest Soul

AKC Breed Popularity No. 3
Temperament Friendly, intelligent, devoted **Average Size** 21.5-24 inches, 55-75 pounds **Activity Level** Energetic **Shedding** Seasonal **Trainability** Eager to please **Life Expectancy** 10-12 years

The golden retriever's name may reference its gorgeous coat, but it could easily describe the breed's joyous disposition. As one of the most popular breeds, its positive traits are endless: The golden is loyal, smart, obedient and playful. These attributes are why the breed makes not only an ideal service dog but also the perfect pet. "Their exceptional temperaments make them wonderful family companions," raves Waterfront Golden Retrievers breeder Amanda Brumley. Like most sporting breeds, the golden is energetic and needs lots of exercise, with swimming and fetching being two of its natural activities. To the golden, anything that allows it to bond with its owner will keep it happy and healthy. "They are highly intelligent, trainable, trustworthy dogs who aim to please their owners," adds Brumley. "The golden retriever truly is a remarkable breed."

Gordon Setter
Biggest Softie

AKC Breed Popularity No. 115
Temperament Affectionate, confident, bold **Average Size** 23-27 inches, 45-80 pounds **Activity Level** Energetic **Shedding** Seasonal **Trainability** Independent **Life Expectancy** 12-13 years

The Gordon setter was bred to withstand the Scottish Highland's tough terrain, but the dog is a total softie and loves nothing more than curling up at its owner's feet. Although keenly intelligent, it can also be stubborn. And when paired with its instinctive drive to run, it's vital to train a puppy to understand basic commands: It must "come" when called, know its name and obey when told "no." While the Gordon setter does require lots of exercise, it will do fine living in an apartment, if that's balanced with physical activity—which should not happen 30 minutes before or after a meal.

Grand Basset Griffon Vendéen
Tireless Energy

AKC Breed Popularity No. 177
Temperament Independent, happy, outgoing **Average Size** 15.5-18 inches, 40-45 pounds **Activity Level** Energetic **Shedding** Seasonal **Trainability** Agreeable **Life Expectancy** 13-15 years

One of the newest breeds to be recognized by the AKC, the grand basset griffon Vendéen is a little dog

DID YOU KNOW? Contrary to popular belief, English, Gordon and Irish setters are three distinct breeds.

Gordon Setter

Grand Basset Griffon Vendéen

with a big name and personality. Active and outgoing, the French scent hound doesn't tire easily and requires an owner to match its stamina. The GBGV needs a yard to run around in, something it will enjoy for many years, since the breed doesn't slow down with age and is typically active well into its teens. Bluntly put, the grand basset griffon Vendéen isn't for someone who's looking for a couch companion—although it is docile and quiet when indoors.

Great Dane
Gentle Giant

AKC Breed Popularity No. 16
Temperament Friendly, patient, dependable **Average Size** 28-32 inches, 110-175 pounds **Activity Level** Energetic **Shedding** Seasonal **Trainability** Agreeable **Life Expectancy** 7-10 years

The Great Dane is known for its size: When standing on its hind legs, it towers over most people! Yet

Great Pyrenees

despite its intimidating stature, it has one of the sweetest dispositions of all breeds and exhibits incredible patience with kids. With its courageous spirit and devotion to protect its family, the Great Dane also makes for a formidable guard dog. With any breed this large, regular exercise is a must, even if it's just a brisk walk two or three times a day. Any activity that's more strenuous, like jogging or hiking, should wait until the dog has reached 2 years of age, to avoid damage to its growing joints. Also because of its size, obedience training is crucial for the Great Dane. Those interested in the breed should be aware of its No. 1 killer: bloat, a condition in which the stomach distends and twists. To reduce the chances of this happening, the dog must not partake in any vigorous exercise before or after meals—and some experts suggest substituting breakfast and dinner with multiple small meals a day as an extra precaution.

Great Pyrenees
🏅 Most Zen
AKC Breed Popularity No. 66 **Temperament** Smart, patient, calm **Average Size** 25–32 inches, 85 pounds and up **Activity Level** Energetic **Shedding** Seasonal **Trainability** Independent **Life Expectancy** 10–12 years

For a large dog, the Great Pyrenees is the picture of grace, serenity and quiet dignity. So many of the breed's traits come from its origins guarding sheep, when it would sit atop a mountain for days. Today, the breed remains a vigilant yet still mellow guardian of its home. And it's relatively undemanding: It needs only moderate exercise, and its coat is resistant to dirt and tangles.

Greater Swiss Mountain Dog
🏅 Most Majestic
AKC Breed Popularity No. 74 **Temperament** Faithful, family-oriented, dependable **Average Size** 23.5–28.5 inches, 85–140 pounds **Activity Level** Energetic **Shedding** Seasonal **Trainability** Agreeable **Life Expectancy** 8–11 years

Strong, agile and dependable, the greater Swiss mountain dog is a worker through and through. In addition to herding flocks around a mountain, it even specialized in hauling carts full of meat and dairy to the market. Despite being an energetic dog, moderate exercise in the form of a walk around the block and the occasional hike is just fine; the breed isn't suitable for someone looking for a running or biking partner. It's important to note that a harness is not recommended to use, as the greater Swiss mountain dog is a draft breed (one that was bred to pull carts) and will instinctively pull much harder on the leash.

Greyhound
🏅 Biggest Couch Potato
AKC Breed Popularity No. 145 **Temperament** Gentle, independent, noble **Average Size** 27–30 inches, 60–70 pounds **Activity Level** Energetic **Shedding** Occasional **Trainability** Independent **Life Expectancy** 10–13 years

The fastest dog (and second-fastest land animal after the cheetah), the greyhound is literally built for speed—from its aerodynamic skull and lean body to the shock-absorbing pads on its feet. Because of its natural-born ability, the breed is typically associated with racing. But in reality, the sensitive and affectionate dog would much rather be curled up on the couch next to its owner. Still, the greyhound does need regular exercise and should be allowed to occasionally run full-out in an enclosed area, either with other canine friends or for a game of fetch. Where do they get all that energy? A diet higher in calories and protein than the average dog is necessary to maintain the health of this unique and fascinating breed.

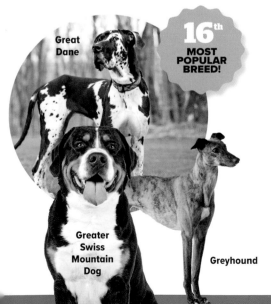

16th MOST POPULAR BREED!

Great Dane

Greater Swiss Mountain Dog

Greyhound

Harrier

H

Harrier
♚ Powerful Hound

AKC Breed Popularity No. 189
Temperament Friendly, people-oriented **Average Size** 19–21 inches, 45–60 pounds **Activity Level** Regular exercise **Shedding** Occasional **Trainability** Easy
Life Expectancy 12–15 years

A relative of the beagle and the English foxhound, the harrier is one of the AKC's rarest breeds, yet has been in America since Colonial times. Because it was developed specifically to spend hours hunting hares (hence its name), the working pack hound requires an ample amount of daily exercise. Without it, the harrier will be bored and could get destructive. Taking long walks or hikes (always securely on a leash) or even participating in canine sports, like tracking or course training, is a good idea. Early socialization with other dogs and puppy classes are recommended since the harrier, although loving and sweet, can be stubborn by nature. Just make sure to take a calm and patient approach, while also being firm, for the best results.

Havanese
♚ Lively Lapdog

AKC Breed Popularity No. 24
Temperament Intelligent, outgoing, funny **Average Size** 8.5–11.5 inches, 7–13 pounds **Activity Level** Regular exercise **Shedding** Occasional **Trainability** Easy
Life Expectancy 14–16 years

Similar to the bichon frise and Maltese, the Havanese is the ideal "little white dog" (although it's not just white). Cheerful, sociable and adaptable, with only moderate exercise needs, the breed is becoming more popular for city dwellers and makes an excellent watchdog. The Havanese is a people-pleaser and can be sensitive, so don't scold too harshly. It loves attention and is happiest when with its owner and shouldn't be left alone for long. The breed's long, silky coat must be brushed multiple times a week to prevent tangles, in addition to wiping its eyes daily to prevent tear stains. A dog as extroverted as the Havanese should look its best!

DID YOU KNOW?
Havanese came to the U.S. from Cuba, when people fleeing Fidel Castro brought the breed with them.

I

Ibizan Hound

Ibizan Hound
♚ Most Graceful

AKC Breed Popularity No. 152
Temperament Family-oriented, even-tempered, polite **Average Size** 22.5–27.5 inches, 45–50 pounds
Activity Level High **Shedding** Occasional **Trainability** Independent
Life Expectancy 11–14 years

One of the most ancient breeds, the Ibizan hound is a timeless beauty with its lithe body, long legs and large, pricked ears. Its unique appearance is often described as deerlike and aids in its natural ability to sprint and leap (it's not uncommon for an Ibizan hound to jump 5 or 6 feet from a standing position). Because of this athleticism, the breed requires a lot of daily exercise, whether that means playing vigorously with its owner or with another dog in a yard with a tall, secure fence; acting as a companion for a regular jogger; or participating in canine sports. The Ibizan hound is also very family-oriented and is devoted to protecting its people, always keeping a watchful eye out for strangers.

Havanese

Icelandic Sheepdog
🏅 **Best Expression**
AKC Breed Popularity No. 155
Temperament Friendly, playful, inquisitive. **Average Size** 16.5–18 inches, 25-30 pounds **Activity Level** Energetic **Shedding** Seasonal **Trainability** Eager to please **Life Expectancy** 12-14 years

Known as the "dog of the Vikings" 1,100 years ago, the Icelandic sheepdog's drive to be faithful to its owners remains as strong today—and its devotion is written all over its face. One of the dog's most endearing traits is its expressive mug, which always appears friendly and happy. The only time the dog is not is when it's left alone for long periods—it loves to be the center of attention. While fairly energetic, only moderate exercise is needed to keep the breed happy and healthy.

Irish Red and White Setter
🏅 **Most Spirited**
AKC Breed Popularity No. 146
Temperament Courageous, spirited, determined **Average Size** 22.5-26 inches, 35-60 pounds **Activity Level** Energetic **Shedding** Occasional **Trainability** Easy **Life Expectancy** 11-15 years

Irish Red and White Setter

Short and stockier than its cousin the Irish setter, the Irish red and white setter is just as friendly and fun-loving—but much more spirited. And if that high energy isn't channeled into lots of daily exercise, the dog will become very challenging. Puppies, though, should only do low-impact activity (no jogging or biking) until they're 18 months old in order to protect their still-developing joints. Training from an early age is a must, although sessions should be kept brief and involve lots of praise. Making its owner happy is what the Irish red and white strives for!

Irish Setter
🏅 **Flashiest Coat**
AKC Breed Popularity No. 77
Temperament Active, outgoing, sweet-natured **Average Size** 25-27 inches, 60-70 pounds **Activity Level** Energetic **Shedding** Occasional **Trainability** Agreeable **Life Expectancy** 12-15 years

An all-around great family dog, the Irish setter understands when to be a rambunctious playmate to children and when to be a sweet companion to older folks—which is why it makes an ideal therapy dog. The breed is most recognizable for its rich red coat, which looks like it would require a lot of care, but only needs to be brushed twice a week (plus the occasional shampoo) to look clean and healthy. Although quite elegant, it's also a high-spirited hunting partner and

Irish Terrier

Icelandic Sheepdog

Irish Setter

requires plenty of exercise if not out in the field. The extra energy can be burned off with long daily walks, play sessions or even canine sports. After all, the Irish setter is just a big kid at heart!

Irish Terrier
🏅 **Littlest Daredevil**
AKC Breed Popularity No. 116
Temperament Tenderhearted, bold, dashing **Average Size** 18 inches, 25-27 pounds **Activity Level** Average **Shedding** Occasional **Trainability** Agreeable **Life Expectancy** 13-15 years

The Irish terrier's disposition is as fiery as its red coat! The little daredevil is willful and outgoing and has an abundance of energy that needs to be burned off with regular exercise—ideally, several walks a day. Another option is agility or hunting events, which also provide an outlet for its athleticism and intelligence. Training can prove tricky, since the breed is strong-willed but also eager to please. Once trained, the Irish terrier and its owner will share a special bond that lasts a lifetime.

Irish Water Spaniel

Irish Water Spaniel

🏅 Best Hair

AKC Breed Popularity No. 159
Temperament Playful, hardworking, brave **Average Size** 21-24 inches, 45-68 pounds **Activity Level** Energetic **Shedding** Infrequent **Trainability** Easy **Life Expectancy** 12-13 years

One of the best swimmers in the canine world, the Irish water spaniel was originally bred strictly to retrieve waterfowl as early as the Renaissance (14th to 17th centuries). These days, the hypoallergenic breed is probably best recognized for its distinctive wavy coat, which crowns the head in an abundance of loose curls. Of course, a coat like this requires special care—and regular grooming should begin when the dog is a puppy so it grows accustomed to weekly gentle brushing, in addition to trimming and reshaping every two months. An active breed, the Irish water spaniel also needs lots of daily exercise, be it long walks or playing with other dogs, so that once it's inside the home, it's calm and relaxed—and on the receiving end of lots of well-deserved affection from its human companion.

Irish Wolfhound

🏅 Gentle Giant

AKC Breed Popularity No. 76
Temperament Courageous, dignified, calm **Average Size** 30-32 inches minimum, 105-120 pounds **Activity Level** Average **Shedding** Seasonal **Trainability** Independent **Life Expectancy** 6-8 years

Don't judge a book by its cover— and don't think the size of the Irish wolfhound means it will make an aggressive guard dog (although its intimidating appearance would certainly be enough to scare off any intruder). The calm, kind breed—and the tallest recognized by the AKC— would much rather snuggle up with its human companions, including children (with supervision), than protect them from danger. The gentle giant is also incredibly sensitive, making it perfect for therapy work as well. As expected with a dog of this size, the Irish wolfhound needs a fair amount of exercise, as long as it's either on a leash or in a fenced-in yard. Until it reaches maturity, at around 18 months old, the puppy (which can weigh as much as 100 pounds) can be destructive if left alone for long periods of time. But as an adult, the dog is prone to becoming a couch potato.

Italian Greyhound

🏅 Littlest Couch Potato

AKC Breed Popularity No. 73
Temperament Playful, alert, sensitive **Average Size** 13-15 inches, 7-14 pounds **Activity Level** Regular exercise **Shedding** Seasonal **Trainability** Independent **Life Expectancy** 14-15 years

A mini version of the greyhound, the Italian greyhound may seem delicate, but it's quite sturdy for such a little dog. And just like its full-size counterpart, the IG is a natural sprinter—yet the affectionate dog would much rather be curled up next to its owner, if not in their lap. Some 2,000 years ago, the IG was bred to be a doting companion, and that instinct has not lessened; it still commands attention today. Although its short coat doesn't require grooming beyond an occasional bath, special care must be taken of its teeth, which should be brushed regularly. Training can prove challenging, especially housebreaking, as the IG is stubborn and sensitive—but with a yummy treat and lots of praise, progress can be made!

Japanese Chin

Japanese Chin

🏅 Smarty Pants

AKC Breed Popularity No. 104
Temperament Charming, noble, loving **Average Size** 8-11 inches, 7-11 pounds **Activity Level** Average **Shedding** Seasonal **Trainability** Independent **Life Expectancy** 10-12 years

Originally bred as companions for royalty, the Japanese Chin's natural instinct is to amuse and charm its owners—and warm their laps. But the breed is more complex than that:

Irish Wolfhound

Italian Greyhound

DID YOU KNOW? Italian greyhounds were favored by 16th-century Italians and appear in Renaissance paintings.

It's not only incredibly smart and stubborn, which can make it tricky to train, but it's also fairly active for a small dog. Slow walks or exploring its fenced yard should suffice though. Another misconception is that its long, silky coat, which gives off an air of aristocracy, is high-maintenance. But it requires only weekly brushing and a monthly bath—making the Japanese Chin an all-around desirable breed.

K

Keeshond
🏅 **Fluffiest**
AKC Breed Popularity No. 95
Temperament Friendly, lively
Average Size 17-18 inches, 35-45 pounds **Activity Level** Average
Shedding Seasonal **Trainability** Easy
Life Expectancy 12-15 years

Similar in look to the Pomeranian, the Keeshond is a spitz with the abundantly poofy coat to prove it. Yet this breed has one more distinctive physical trait: the shading around its eyes that looks like it's wearing spectacles, which highlights its amiable expression. The Keeshond is also incredibly adaptable, although no matter whether it lives in the city or out in the country, the dog requires regular daily exercise—preferably with its human, who it will want to cuddle up next to once back at home. The Keeshond is also so bright and quick to learn, it could train in agility or even as a therapy dog.

Kerry Blue Terrier
🏅 **Show Stopper**
AKC Breed Popularity No. 129
Temperament Smart, alert, people-oriented **Average Size** 17.5-19.5 inches, 30-40 pounds **Activity Level** Average **Shedding** Infrequent
Trainability May be stubborn
Life Expectancy 12-15 years

Although bred to be a farm dog, the Kerry blue terrier has evolved

Keeshond

Kerry Blue Terrier

into one of the canine world's biggest showstoppers. Surprisingly, its unmistakable blue coat doesn't shed (although it must be brushed to prevent matting), making the breed ideal for those who suffer from allergies. The adaptable Kerry blue tends to have two speeds: It will either want to play at full speed or relax on the couch. Either way, it wants to be with its humans—and, in return, will be a devoted watchdog.

Komondor
🏅 **Funkiest Appearance**
AKC Breed Popularity No. 173
Temperament Loyal, dignified
Average Size 25.5-27.5 inches, 80-100 pounds or more **Activity Level** Average **Shedding** Infrequent
Trainability Independent
Life Expectancy 10-12 years

Much like the puli and Bergamesco, the komondor is characterized by a white dreadlocked coat, which allowed it to blend in with the sheep it was guarding. Despite appearances, the cords don't smell, as long as shampoo (which should be diluted) is thoroughly rinsed out. Because of its inherent agility, sufficient exercise is necessary, especially a free run in a fenced-in yard. But a dog park is not a good idea—its guardian instincts may cause it to react badly to a loose strange dog. For its size, the komondor doesn't eat much and is known to skip meals.

Komondor

Kuvasz

Kuvasz

♀ Dignified Guardian

AKC Breed Popularity No. 163
Temperament Loyal, fearless, sweet
Average Size 26–30 inches, 70–115
pounds **Activity Level** Average
Shedding Regular
Trainability Independent
Life Expectancy 10–12 years

More than 500 years ago, the kuvasz acted as both protector of its flock and companion to royalty—and all these centuries later, its job description is pretty much the same (although now it's more likely to guard its humans and home). The impressive and imposing dog is profoundly loyal and patient—the same qualities potential owners must exhibit when training a kuvasz. The independent breed tends to mature more slowly than others, which could prove challenging to some novice dog owners. Just be sure to utilize positive training methods, as the dog is sensitive and also wants to please its family.

Labrador Retriever

♀ Most Popular

AKC Breed Popularity No. 1
Temperament Friendly, active,

outgoing **Average Size** 21.5–24.5
inches, 55–80 pounds **Activity
Level** Energetic **Shedding** Regular
Trainability Eager to please
Life Expectancy 10–12 years

The mold was broken with the Labrador retriever. Famously intelligent, affectionate, loyal and enthusiastic, it's no wonder the dog has been favored since the early 1800s—and has been the No. 1 AKC breed for 20-plus years. Whether you're a first-time dog owner or a family looking to add a compatible four-legged member, the Lab (which comes in three colors: yellow, black and chocolate) is a surefire selection. "What I love most about the Labrador retriever is its levelheadedness, sensible temperament and love for all," says Barbara Gilchrist, who sits on the board of directors for the Labrador Retriever Club. "This breed is easily trained and so very biddable that any person with a beginner level of dog experience can raise a Labrador puppy successfully."

As a sporting breed, the Lab does need daily exercise. Without it, adds Gilchrist, "the pup will find its own ways of doing things, which won't be good. A large backyard is great, but even with that, they love their families, so being turned outside to play on their own is not the answer. They are a social breed that wants to be part of the family, going with them everywhere." Beyond being a lovable pet that is trustworthy with kids, Labs are also used in search-

Labrador
Retriever

1st MOST POPULAR BREED!

and-rescue and bomb-detection missions and as service dogs. "There is not much a Lab cannot be trained to do," adds Gilchrist. "They can go out at dawn and retrieve ducks and geese in freezing-cold weather and then sleep on your 8-year-old child's bed that night." When selecting a puppy, Gilchrist recommends visiting the breeder's kennel and meeting the litter's parents, if possible. "[Breeders] should be doing all the clearances on their breeding dogs to help ensure that the puppies are given the best chance of being free of hip and elbow dysplasia, plus a cardiac clearance, a current eye exam and some genetic screening."

Lagotto Romagnolo

♀ Cutest Curls

AKC Breed Popularity No. 99
Temperament Affectionate, keen,
undemanding **Average Size** 16–19
inches, 24–35 pounds **Activity Level**
Average **Shedding** Infrequent
Trainability Eager to please **Life
Expectancy** 15–17 years

Italy's most celebrated breed is more than an adorable fluff of curls. The lagotto Romagnolo uses its nose to

Lagotto
Romagnolo

sniff out pricey truffles as well as to aid in search-and-rescue tasks. Its teddy bear–like coat sheds very little and is easy to maintain with regular trims and brushing. Lively but not hyper, the intelligent dog does require moderate activity as well as mental stimulation to stay healthy and happy.

Lakeland Terrier
🏵 **Biggest Little Dog**

AKC Breed Popularity No. 147
Temperament Friendly, confident, bold
Average Size 14-15 inches or smaller, 17 pounds **Activity Level** Average
Shedding Infrequent
Trainability Agreeable
Life Expectancy 12-15 years

Similar in physical appearance to the Kerry blue terrier, the Lakeland terrier is about half the size—but don't be fooled. It has a bold, big-dog personality, with plenty of swagger. Exercise is as important to the breed's mind as it is its body, and free running is recommended (in a secured area), as opposed to walks on a short leash. Training is also vital for the highly intelligent Lakeland, as long as the sessions are not boring and repetitive. The dog is simply too smart for ordinary training classes!

Leonberger
🏵 **Most Majestic**

AKC Breed Popularity No. 93
Temperament Friendly, gentle, playful **Average Size** 25.5-31.5 inches, 90-170 pounds **Activity Level** Average
Shedding Frequent **Trainability** Eager to please **Life Expectancy** 7 years

Originally created to be a pet for royalty, the Leonberger is truly fit for a king, with its majestic leonine mane and gentle, patient nature. The breed's grace and elegance is as big as its stature, and it moves surprisingly well for such a large dog. And because a full-grown Leonberger will likely outweigh its humans, it's imperative that puppies receive obedience training, preferably in a group, in addition to proper socialization with people and animals, before they reach 20 weeks. Also, because of the breed's size, a Leonberger isn't recommended for those living in an apartment or small house. Although generally a calm dog, it will need space to play. Another note to owners: Leonbergers shed quite a bit and should be brushed daily to prevent matting, in addition to weekly grooming to rake out the undercoat.

Leonberger

Lakeland Terrier

Best Breeds for Kids

Most children love dogs—but the same can't be said for most dogs. Some don't thrive on kids' high energy, while others don't know their own size and can accidentally knock over little ones. It's important to select a breed that's patient, playful (but knows when to be gentle) and isn't easily spooked by loud noises. According to the AKC, these are the 13 best breeds for kids.

Australian Terrier	Boxer	Newfoundland
Basset Fauve de Bretagne	Bracco Italiano	Soft-Coated Wheaten Terrier
Beagle	Bull Terrier	Spanish Mastiff
Beauceron	Golden Retriever	Weimaraner
	Labrador Retriever	

155

Lhasa Apso

Lhasa Apso

Family Comedian

AKC Breed Popularity No. 71
Temperament Confident, smart, comical **Average Size** 10-11 or smaller inches, 12-18 pounds **Activity Level** Average **Shedding** Infrequent **Trainability** Independent **Life Expectancy** 12-15 years

The Lhasa apso is probably best known for a floor-length coat, parted in the middle—but it's got more than just exotic good looks. To enthusiasts, the breed is highly intelligent, creative, merry and especially comical with its family (strangers, on the other hand, get the cold shoulder). Stubborn with training, the Lhasa apso is also independent with exercise and is perfectly happy running around the house or a fenced-in yard to burn off energy. The breed's lavish coat does require special care—whether it's kept long or in a puppy cut—with regular brushing and bathing in between visits to the groomer.

DID YOU KNOW?
Lhasa apsos are known for their long life expectancy—the oldest one reportedly lived to age 29!

Löwchen

Little Charmer

AKC Breed Popularity No. 168
Temperament Affectionate, outgoing, positive **Average Size** 12-14 inches, 15 pounds **Activity Level** Average **Shedding** Occasional **Trainability** Agreeable **Life Expectancy** 13-15 years

Another breed that was originally developed to be a companion to European royals, the löwchen is quite the little charmer. Lively and affectionate, there's a big heart inside that little body. Despite its size, the breed is remarkably sturdy and enjoys long walks and romps in the yard—just don't expect the dog to accompany you on vigorous jogs. Still, with its keen intellect and fairly easy trainability, the löwchen is an excellent candidate for obedience and agility activities, where it can really show its stuff.

Löwchen

M

Maltese

Maltese

Smallest Watchdog

AKC Breed Popularity No. 37
Temperament Gentle, playful, charming **Average Size** 7-9 inches, under 7 pounds **Activity Level** Average **Shedding** Infrequent **Trainability** Agreeable **Life Expectancy** 12-15 years

Between the showstopping white coat, intelligence, elegance and affection, it's no surprise that the Maltese has been captivating fans since the fourth century B.C.—which also means it's had plenty of time to practice manipulating humans to get what it wants. The Maltese's big, dark eyes are easy to get lost in, which is why it's important to establish leadership with consistent training as a puppy. Although prone to being stubborn, positive, reward-based methods can help do the trick. The teacup pup is also rather sturdy and a remarkably fearless watchdog.

Miniature American Shepherd

Miniature Bull Terrier

Manchester Terrier

Mastiff

Manchester Terrier
♜ Sleek & Solid
AKC Breed Popularity No. 133
Temperament Spirited, bright, observant **Average Size** 15-16 inches, 12-22 pounds (standard); 10-12 inches, under 12 pounds (toy) **Activity Level** Average **Shedding** Occasional **Trainability** Easy **Life Expectancy** 15-17 years

Whether standard or toy, the Manchester terrier is a sleek, swift, intelligent and fearless dog. In fact, the only difference between the two, other than size, is ear shape. Both are quite athletic and should be taken on a couple of daily walks, in addition to a game of fetch so it can show off its speed. And since the Manchester terrier is also easily trainable, it's an ideal candidate for canine sports. Its jet-black-and-mahogany coat is wash-and-wear, although the dog's ears should be cleaned regularly to prevent infection—luckily, it sees grooming sessions as time to bond with its human companion.

Mastiff
♜ Most Colossal
AKC Breed Popularity No. 37
Temperament Courageous, dignified, good-natured **Average Size** 27.5 inches

and up, 120-230 pounds **Activity Level** Average **Shedding** Seasonal **Trainability** Agreeable **Life Expectancy** 6-10 years

At nearly twice the size of the massive bullmastiff, the mastiff is one of the canine world's most colossal members. In fact, during the Roman Empire, the breed was used to battle wild beasts and human gladiators in the arena. Yet as hulking as it appears, the dog is remarkably docile—but strangers wouldn't know that when they lay eyes on such a formidable protector. Although wary of those it doesn't know, with its family, the mastiff is endlessly loving and loyal (albeit, also pretty drooly). In return, it needs moderate exercise, about a mile or two of walking daily for adult dogs, which means it can live happily in an apartment or small home. Of course, with a dog of the mastiff's powerful stature, ownership is a commitment that cannot be taken lightly—and early obedience training is a must.

Miniature American Shepherd
♜ Endlessly Loyal
AKC Breed Popularity No. 34
Temperament Good-natured, intelligent, devoted **Average Size** 13-18 inches, 20-40 pounds **Activity Level** Average **Shedding** Regular **Trainability** Eager to please **Life Expectancy** 12-13 years

Resembling the very popular Australian shepherd in appearance and temperament, the miniature

American shepherd shares all the same attributes, like intelligence and athleticism—just in a dog half the size. Similarly, the breed is loyal and devoted to its humans and adaptable to their lifestyle, whether it's in the city or the country, so long as it gets sufficient daily exercise to remain healthy and happy.

Miniature Bull Terrier
♜ Little Clown
AKC Breed Popularity No. 110
Temperament Upbeat, mischievous, comical **Average Size** 10-14 inches, 18-28 pounds **Activity Level** Energetic **Shedding** Seasonal **Trainability** Independent **Life Expectancy** 11-13 years

Although not as popular as its full-size counterpart, the miniature bull terrier shares many of its same traits, especially its tendency to be mischievous and comical, as well as its egg-shaped head. Special care must be taken with a puppy to ensure it will be a healthy and happy adult dog—not only with obedience training but also with exercise. While energetic, the miniature bull terrier can be prone to "sudden lameness," the result of rapid growth rate and constantly being in motion—an intricacy the breed typically outgrows when fully matured.

Miniature Pinscher
♔ King of Toys
AKC Breed Popularity No. 70
Temperament Fearless, fun-loving, proud **Average Size** 10-12.5 inches, 8-10 pounds **Activity Level** Average
Shedding Regularly
Trainability Independent
Life Expectancy 12-16 years

Often mistaken as a toy Doberman pinscher, the miniature pinscher is a cross between a dachshund and an Italian greyhound. Considered the king of all toy breeds, the leggy min-pin is distinguished by its high-stepping gait, reminiscent of a trotting horse. But make no mistake: The fearless and fun-loving dog is all canine and at its best when properly exercised with multiple walks a day or chasing after a ball—balanced out with relaxing at home with its beloved human.

Miniature Pinscher

70th MOST POPULAR BREED!

Miniature Schnauzer

Neapolitan Mastiff

N

Miniature Schnauzer
♔ Ideal Family Dog
AKC Breed Popularity No. 19
Temperament Friendly, active, outgoing **Average Size** 12-14 inches, 11-20 pounds **Activity Level** Average **Shedding** Infrequent
Trainability Eager to please
Life Expectancy 12-15 years

The smallest of the three schnauzers, the miniature is also the most popular—and one of the top breeds in the canine world. Beloved for its friendliness, trainability, intellect, tireless devotion and capacity to get along with both children and other animals, the miniature schnauzer is an ideal all-around family pet. And with its medium energy level, the breed is an especially good choice for those who live in an apartment or small home. Although its double coat (a wiry topcoat with a soft undercoat) does require frequent brushing in between professional groomings, the dog is actually low-shedding.

Neapolitan Mastiff
♔ Biggest Head
AKC Breed Popularity No. 102
Temperament Loyal, dignified, watchful **Average Size** 24-31 inches, 110-150 pounds **Activity Level** Average **Shedding** Regularly
Trainability May be stubborn
Life Expectancy 7-9 years

Of all the mastiffs, the Neapolitan stands apart, with its profusely wrinkly appearance. To strangers, it's an imposing watchdog punctuated by a massive head. Yet to its loving family, the breed is 100-plus pounds of sweetness and loyalty. Due to its massive size and power, obedience training is an absolute must with the Neapolitan mastiff. Other precautions must also be taken with this special breed: It's not recommended to play tug-of-war or wrestle with the dog, and care should be taken when romping outside in warm weather, as it can overheat easily.

Nederlandse
Kooikerhondje

Nederlandse Kooikerhondje

🏅 **Biggest Heart**

AKC Breed Popularity No. 150
Temperament Friendly, attentive, quick-witted **Average Size** 15-16 inches, 20-30 pounds **Activity Level** Average **Shedding** Seasonal **Trainability** Eager to please **Life Expectancy** 12-15 years

Known as the "little white-and-orange dog with a big heart," the Nederlandse kooikerhondje is true to its name. The breed is beloved for being good-natured, cheerful and friendly, particularly in the home. Let the dog outdoors, though, and its instincts as an athletic and energetic hard worker kick into overdrive—yet it's not hyperactive. With its intelligence and eager-to-please attitude, the Nederlandse kooikerhondje is easy to train into the sweetest companion.

Newfoundland

🏅 **Sterling Character**

AKC Breed Popularity No. 40
Temperament Sweet, patient, devoted **Average Size** 26-28 inches, 100-150 pounds **Activity Level** Average **Shedding** Seasonal **Trainability** Easy **Life Expectancy** 9-10 years

Dogs don't get much sweeter than the Newfoundland. The above-and-beyond protector does not have an aggressive bone in its body. In fact, it's so gentle and patient, the Newfoundland has

Newfoundland

earned the reputation of "nanny dog" for its family's kids. Naturally, with a dog of this size, regular activity is a must to keep its mind and body healthy with at least 30 minutes of exercise daily—which can be anything from a long walk or hike to a swim. But like many large breeds, the Newfoundland can experience bloat, so vigorous activity around meals should be avoided. A helpful tip is to instead feed it multiple small meals per day.

Norfolk Terrier

🏅 **Ideal Travel Buddy**

AKC Breed Popularity No. 126
Temperament Fearless, alert, fun-loving **Average Size** 9-10 inches, 11-12 pounds **Activity Level** Average **Shedding** Infrequent **Trainability** Agreeable **Life Expectancy** 12-16 years

A terrier through and through, the Norfolk is feisty, confident and game for whatever adventure its human companion has in mind. These qualities, along with its adaptability, make the breed a good little travel buddy. Even if you two don't hit the road together,

Norfolk Terrier

Norwegian Buhund

the Norfolk terrier will form a tight bond with its owner, so it's important that the dog be included in family activities—after all, it was originally bred to work in a pack.

Norwegian Buhund

🏅 **Biggest Homebody**

AKC Breed Popularity No. 165
Temperament Confident, smart, perceptive **Average Size** 16-18.5 inches, 26-40 pounds **Activity Level** Energetic **Shedding** Seasonal **Trainability** Easy **Life Expectancy** 12-15 years

Once the loyal companions to Vikings, the Norwegian buhund is now a devoted and affectionate family dog that has a special affinity for children. An active home in which it can run and play is ideal for the energetic medium-size breed, which was originally developed to work for long hours at a time on its owner's property (hence its name, *bu*, which means "homestead" in Norwegian). Highly intelligent (and food-motivated), the Norwegian buhund is easily trainable. Another plus: The double-coated dog is naturally clean and basically odorless, even when wet.

Norwegian Elkhound

Norwegian Lundehund

Norwich Terrier

Nova Scotia Duck Tolling Retriever

curious **Average Size** 10 inches, 12 pounds **Activity Level** Average **Shedding** Infrequent **Trainability** Agreeable **Life Expectancy** 12-15 years

Norwegian Elkhound

🏅 **Best Beggar**

AKC Breed Popularity No. 97
Temperament Confident, dependable
Average Size 19.5-20.5 inches, 48-55 pounds **Activity Level** Average
Shedding Occasional
Trainability Agreeable
Life Expectancy 12-15 years

One of Europe's oldest dogs, the Norwegian elkhound got its start sailing with Vikings. On land, it was a moose tracker for hunters. Due to this instinct, it's important for the elkhound to trot for miles from time to time, in addition to regular daily activity. At home, it's an intelligent and trustworthy friend. Just don't fall for its puppy-dog eyes: The "food hound" is notorious for making a pitiful face to get extra treats or table scraps from humans.

Norwegian Lundehund

🏅 **Most Flexible**

AKC Breed Popularity No. 191
Temperament Loyal, energetic, alert
Average Size 12-15 inches, 20-30 pounds **Activity Level** Average
Shedding Seasonal **Trainability** Agreeable **Life Expectancy** 12-15 year

The smallest of the Norwegian breeds, the lundehund is also the most unique. The only dog created to hunt puffin, a seabird with a brightly colored beak, it has an impressive body constructed for the job: an "elastic neck" that allows it to tip its head backward and touch its backbone, ears that fold shut and forelegs that extend perpendicular to the body, giving it a distinctive "rotary" gait.
Though the puffin is now a protected species, the modern Norwegian lundehund is a clever, affectionate and fun-loving dog with a high energy level that requires daily exercise, such as taking a brisk 30-minute walk or chasing a ball around the yard with its owner.

DID YOU KNOW?
Since 1953, the Norwegian lundehund has six fully functioning toes on each foot, as well as extra paw pads.

Norwich Terrier

🏅 **Most Jovial**

AKC Breed Popularity No. 108
Temperament Affectionate, loyal,

Among the smallest of working terriers, the Norwich terrier is a big dog in a cute little package: fearless, tough, spirited and happy-go-lucky. Energetic enough to play all day, it requires ample exercise and should always be on-leash, due to its high hunting instincts. At home, the breed—which is physically similar to the Norfolk terrier, but distinguishable by its erect ears—is content to cuddle up in its owner's lap for hours on end.

Nova Scotia Duck Tolling Retriever

🏅 **Cutest Redhead**

AKC Breed Popularity No. 83
Temperament Affectionate, intelligent, outgoing **Average Size** 17-21 inches, 35-50 pounds **Activity Level** Energetic **Shedding** Seasonal **Trainability** May be stubborn **Life Expectancy** 12-14 years

The smallest of the AKC retrievers, the Nova Scotia duck tolling retriever is a cunning, agile and loving dog with a handsome crimson coat. Originally bred for duck hunting, they would imitate a fox, tricking ducks into flying into gunshot range. Tollers are athletic and tireless, so owners should arrange daily vigorous exercise, at least a 30-minute brisk walk or ball-chasing session. For those who are more outdoorsy, hiking, camping and swimming are all activities the breed enjoys.

Old English Sheepdog

will bark if it feels its family is being threatened in any way. Because of its size, obedience training is a must to correct any behavior before the puppy grows—luckily, the Old English sheepdog is so smart, once it learns something, it doesn't forget it.

Old English Sheepdog
🏵 **Most Shaggy**
AKC Breed Popularity No. 72
Temperament Adorable, gentle, smart **Average Size** 21 inches and up, 60-100 pounds **Activity Level** Average **Shedding** Seasonal **Trainability** Independent
Life Expectancy 10-12 years

The quintessential shaggy dog, the Old English sheepdog is best known for its profuse and puffy coat—not to mention its adorable bearlike shuffle. But while the breed is large and seemingly clumsy, under all that hair is a muscular, rather agile dog. Although rambunctious when at play, the Old English sheepdog is quite the gentle giant and especially patient and kind with children. But it's also a courageous protector and

Otterhound
🏵 **Most Rare**
AKC Breed Popularity No. 182
Temperament Even-tempered, amiable, boisterous **Average Size** 24-27 inches, 80-115 pounds **Activity Level** Average **Shedding** Occasional **Trainability** May be stubborn
Life Expectancy 10-13 years

The otterhound was so good at its job back in medieval England that the otter nearly went extinct—after which hunting it was outlawed. These days, it's the otterhound that's endangered, with only approximately 800 worldwide (there are more giant pandas that otterhounds). But those who know the breed adore it for its big, bouncy personality and expert swimming skills. These are also the same reasons early training is a must with this breed.

Otterhound

Papillon
🏵 **Dainty Dynamo**
AKC Breed Popularity No. 54
Temperament Friendly, alert, happy
Average Size 8-11 inches, 5-10 pounds
Activity Level Average **Shedding** Seasonal **Trainability** Eager to please
Life Expectancy 14-16 years

Papillon

Don't be fooled by the papillon's dainty appearance—under that long, silky coat and plumed tail is the hardy build of an athlete. The surprisingly robust breed makes for an excellent agility dog. At home, the papillon is just as active: Indoors, it enjoys playing ball, while outdoors, it will just as happily chase after squirrels and insects, no matter the weather. The breed also easily adapts to life in the city or country, as long as it's with its family. The papillon (French for "butterfly," a reference to the shape of its ears) is a companion dog at heart and depends on that bond for its own health and happiness. But its buddy doesn't always have to be human: If your lifestyle keeps you away from the home for long periods, another pet is a good idea so the papillon always has a friend to keep it company.

Parson Russell Terrier
Most Independent

AKC Breed Popularity No. 117
Temperament Friendly, clever, athletic **Average Size** 13-14 inches, 13-17 pounds **Activity Level** Energetic **Shedding** Occasional **Trainability** Agreeable **Life Expectancy** 13-15 years

Often confused with the similar Jack Russell terrier (which isn't recognized by the AKC), the Parson Russell terrier is a bold dog that's fast, fearless and fun-loving, despite its small size. These traits, plus the breed's high energy, must be balanced with lots of exercise, like play sessions in a fenced-in yard (it has a very strong prey drive) and long walks, preferably in the woods, so it can explore and sniff. If you're not fairly active, the breed is not ideal. When properly trained and socialized, the Parson Russell can be wonderful with children, as long as they are gentle—this tough little dog won't tolerate rough handling.

Pekingese
Most Regal

AKC Breed Popularity No. 92
Temperament Affectionate, loyal, regal in manner **Average Size**

6-9 inches, up to 14 pounds **Activity Level** Calm **Shedding** Seasonal **Trainability** May be stubborn **Life Expectancy** 12-14 years

A sacred breed that was exclusive to ancient Chinese royalty, the Pekingese is as loyal as it is sophisticated. Just as in its days living in palaces, the breed is an alert watchdog as well as a comforting companion that will form a tight bond with its favorite human. Its long coat does require a bit of upkeep: Expect to spend an hour per week brushing it—a suitable investment for such a regal creature.

DID YOU KNOW?
In 1912, a Pekingese named Sun Yat-Sen was one of three dogs that survived the sinking of the Titanic.

Pembroke Welsh Corgi
Most Delightful

AKC Breed Popularity No. 13
Temperament Affectionate, smart, alert **Average Size** 10-12 inches, up to 30 pounds **Activity Level** Energetic **Shedding** Regular **Trainability** Agreeable **Life Expectancy** 12-13 years

Similar to the Cardigan Welsh corgi but more popular, the Pembroke Welsh is the physical embodiment of cuteness—from its keen expression and short yet powerful legs right down to its fluffy backside. Sharing your life with a Pembroke is a complete joy: The happy little dog is bright, affectionate, sensitive, playful, loyal and bold.

The breed is also a vigilant protector and has a big-dog bark that backs up its fearlessness. Just ask Prince Harry. "For the last 33 years, I've been barked at," he joked in 2018 about his grandmother Queen Elizabeth II's Pembroke Welsh corgis, which she first got on her 18th birthday. Despite the breed's short and stout build, it's remarkably agile and benefits from daily moderate exercise; just be sure to avoid extreme heat or cold.

Petit Basset Griffon Vendéen
Little Tough Guy

AKC Breed Popularity No. 156
Temperament Alert, happy, vivacious **Average Size** 13-15 inches, 25-40 pounds **Activity Level** Energetic **Shedding** Occasional **Trainability** Independent **Life Expectancy** 14-16 years

The petit basset griffon Vendéen may have small in its name, but it is a robust dog with strong legs, tenacity and a thundering bark,

Pekingese

Parson Russell Terrier

13th MOST POPULAR BREED!

Pembroke Welsh Corgi

Petit Basset Griffon Vendéen

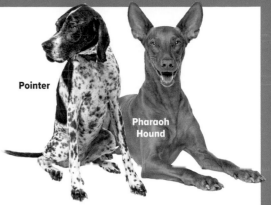

Pointer

Pharaoh Hound

originally bred to hunt rabbits on the rocky West Coast of France. But under that thick, harsh coat, the dog is a happy and vivacious little fellow that deeply loves its family (including children and other pets) as well as its friends. Due to the dog's natural instincts, the petit basset griffon Vendéen must have plenty of space to explore and always be secured on a leash or in a fenced-in area, if outside, as the breed has a strong sense of smell—and the curiosity to follow the trail to the very end.

Pharaoh Hound
♺ Free Spirit
AKC Breed Popularity No. 172
Temperament Friendly, smart, noble **Average Size** 21-25 inches, 45-55 pounds **Activity Level** Energetic
Shedding Seasonal **Trainability** Independent
Life Expectancy 12-14 years

Elegant yet rugged, the ancient pharaoh hound is the perfect combination of tenacious hunter and affectionate family pet. Its aerodynamic body is typical of a hound, but the breed has a few extra perks: stunning amber eyes, the ability to smile, and a unique way of blushing when happy. As expected with a dog of this athleticism and speed, it does need a fair amount of exercise. Preferably, it will be able to run freely in an enclosed area—at minimum, 50 feet by 50 feet, surrounded by a 6-foot-high fence—twice a day for at least 15 minutes each time. If that's not possible, two 20-minute walks will suffice. It's important to stress that no matter how well-trained, a pharaoh hound should never be allowed off-leash in an unsecured environment, as it will not come when called and will instead run off to hunt.

Plott
♺ Most Unique Coonhound
AKC Breed Popularity No. 171
Temperament Loyal, alert, intelligent
Average Size 20-25 inches, 40-60 pounds **Activity Level** Energetic
Shedding Occasional
Trainability Independent
Life Expectancy 12-14 years

Of the six AKC coonhound breeds, the brindle Plott is considered the most unique. Descended from German Hanover hounds, it was bred by immigrant Johannes Plott to hunt bear and boar in 18th-century North Carolina (in 1989, it was named the official state dog). Rugged and relentless on the trail, at home it's a gentle and loving dog that's often wagging its tail. The Plott puppy is intelligent and

Plott

quite energetic and, as a result, demands attention and mental stimulation. Early training and socialization with people and pets is recommended, especially since the Plott can be food- or toy-aggressive.

Pointer
♺ Best Running Partner
AKC Breed Popularity No. 114
Temperament Loyal, hardworking, even-tempered **Average Size** 23-28 inches, 45-75 pounds **Activity Level** Energetic **Shedding** Occasional
Trainability Agreeable
Life Expectancy 12-17 years

Just as its name states, the breed is an expert at pointing (the instinct to find and aim its muzzle toward game birds) while working alongside hunters. The embodiment of power and grace, the pointer is remarkably quick and agile, and it demands an active daily life to burn off energy, making the pointer an ideal companion for runners. An exercised pointer is happy, healthy—and, most important, a calm dog inside the home. With its even temperament and friendly nature, the highly trainable breed can also excel at service and therapy work.

163

Poodle

Polish
Lowland
Sheepdog

Pomeranian

7th MOST POPULAR BREED!

Pomeranian
🏅 **Best Smile**
AKC Breed Popularity No. 23
Temperament Inquisitive, bold, lively **Average Size** 6-7 inches, 3-7 pounds **Activity Level** Average **Shedding** Seasonal **Trainability** Agreeable **Life Expectancy** 12-16 years

What's not to like about the Pomeranian, a tiny dog with a vivacious personality, a foxy face, a glorious coat and the adaptability to live in the city or suburbs—which is why it's one of the most popular toy breeds. Though a lapdog, it does enjoy walks and an occasional romp in the yard. When outdoors, it's important to be alert: Not only can the Pom easily escape through small gaps in fencing, but birds could mistake the pup for prey.

Poodle (Toy/Miniature/Standard)
🏅 **Most Intelligent**
AKC Breed Popularity No. 7
Temperament Active, proud, very

Polish Lowland Sheepdog
🏅 **Quick Learner**
AKC Breed Popularity No. 170
Temperament Confident, clever, lively
Average Size 17-20 inches, 30-50 pounds **Activity Level** Calm **Shedding** Seasonal **Trainability** May be stubborn **Life Expectancy** 12-14 years

For anyone looking for an excellent family dog that's a gentle playmate for small children, an alert guardian of the home and even a buddy to other pets, the Polish lowland sheepdog is a quality choice—especially if it will have access to a fenced-in yard. A high-energy herding dog, the breed should be allowed to run freely for at least an hour or two daily. Additionally, the Polish lowland sheepdog's shaggy double coat requires daily brushing, with a more thorough job done once a week.

smart **Average Size** No more than 10 inches, 4-6 pounds (toy); 10-15 inches, 10-15 pounds (miniature); over 15 inches, 40-70 pounds (standard) **Activity Level** Average **Shedding** Infrequent **Trainability** Eager to please **Life Expectancy** 10-18 years

There's no mistaking the curly-coated poodle. The popular breed comes in three distinct sizes (toy, miniature or standard) and colors (black, white or apricot)—but no matter the combination, the dog promises the same extreme intelligence, sense of humor, athleticism and sheer beauty. "Most toys think they're standards, and the minis know they're the perfect size," jokes Susan Burge, president of the Poodle Club of America. "It is an individual's personal and life choices that determine the best size for them." Given the poodle's impressive brainpower, it's easy to train. Beyond obedience, the people-pleasing breed is also known to excel in canine sports like agility, tracking and dock diving. "Every day, I see poodles doing new skills, always learning," marvels Burge, who does obedience and rallies with her pup, Henry. The high-energy poodle is not afraid to romp around, and all three sizes enjoy a fair amount of activity—preferably with their human. "Regardless if they

DID YOU KNOW?
Although the poodle is the national dog of France, the toy variety was first bred in the U.S. to be a city pet.

are strutting in the show ring, flying high over jumps in obedience or a rally, retrieving ducks during a hunt or merely cuddling on a cold night with a beloved companion, poodles need people," stresses Burge. "If you want a dog that is totally independent, a poodle is not for you."

Portuguese Podengo Pequeño

DID YOU KNOW?
Portuguese water dogs became popular when the Obamas welcomed Bo to the White House in 2009.

Portuguese Water Dog

Best Hypoallergenic Breeds

According to the American College of Allergy, Asthma and Immunology, 10 percent of the U.S. population is allergic to dogs. If you're in that minority, fear not: Although no breed is 100 percent hypoallergenic, there are a handful that don't shed.

Afghan Hound

American Hairless Terrier

Bichon Frise

Coton de Tulear

Schnauzer (Standard and Giant)

Maltese

Poodle (Miniature, Standard and Toy)

Portuguese Water Dog

Portuguese Podengo Pequeño

🏵 **Smallest Hunter**

AKC Breed Popularity No. 154
Temperament Playful, charming, lively **Average Size** 8-12 inches, 9-13 pounds **Activity Level** Average
Shedding Seasonal
Trainability Independent
Life Expectancy 12-15 years

The Portuguese podengo pequeño packs a lot of athleticism and skill into its little body. Considered the world's smallest hunting dog, the energetic breed is tireless, due to its centuries of trailing rabbits back in its homeland. These days, the playful PPP prefers to chase after its humans in a large fenced-in yard in addition to other daily activities, like vigorous walks. Indoors, the breed (its coat comes in either smooth or wiry) is a charming and well-mannered family pet and watchdog.

Portuguese Water Dog

🏵 **Most Eager to Please**

AKC Breed Popularity No. 50
Temperament Affectionate, adventurous, athletic **Average Size**

17-23 inches, 35-60 pounds
Activity Level Energetic **Shedding** Seasonal **Trainability** Easy
Life Expectancy 11-13 years

As the fisherman's right-hand man, the Portuguese water dog was trained to carry out a variety of demanding tasks, such as retrieving lost tackle and acting as a messenger between ships and shore. Over the centuries, the web-toed dog has not lost its title as one of the brightest and most biddable breeds. These days, the Portuguese water dog is just as eager to please its human, although at times it can be demanding of their attention. The dog is known to greet friends and family with such enthusiasm, it might actually be too much for households with small children. The Portuguese water dog is great for those prone to allergies though: Its waterproof coat, which can be wavy or curly, rarely sheds and is hypoallergenic.

Puli

Pumi

Pug

Pumi

Pumi

🏅 **Best Fetcher**

AKC Breed Popularity No. 151
Temperament Intelligent, lively, ready to work **Average Size** 15–18.5 inches, 22–29 pounds **Activity Level** Average **Shedding** Infrequently **Trainability** Agreeable **Life Expectancy** 12–13 years

The Hungarian sheepdog is a descendent of the closely named puli, but it doesn't share the same dreadlocked coat. With corkscrew curls (which can be ruined if a blow-dryer is used on them), the nonshedding pumi stands on its own as a smart and bold dog characterized by a charming expression. Like the puli, the pumi also requires mental stimulation in addition to physical exercise. One of its favorite activities is playing fetch: Throw a tennis ball for the pumi, and you'll have an adorable best friend for life.

Pug

🏅 **Biggest Ham**

AKC Breed Popularity No. 28
Temperament Charming, mischievous, loving **Average Size** 10–13 inches, 14–18 pounds **Activity Level** Average **Shedding** Regular **Trainability** Agreeable **Life Expectancy** 13–15 years

Bred to be a companion to Chinese emperors (and later, Dutch royalty), the pug still lives to please and love its owners. The small yet sturdy dog remains an ideal household pet, versatile enough to thrive in the city or suburbs and, with its even temperament, under the same roof as both young children or older folks. Although the pug is content to spend its day napping, the dog does have a playful side and loves nothing more than to be the center of attention. As with other flat-faced breeds, special attention must be paid so that the pug doesn't engage in strenuous outdoor activity in hot or humid weather.

Puli

🏅 **Funkiest Hair**

AKC Breed Popularity No. 160
Temperament Loyal, smart, home-loving **Average Size** 16–17 inches, 25–35 pounds **Activity Level** Average **Shedding** Infrequent **Trainability** Independent **Life Expectancy** 10–15 years

Very few breeds are as instantly recognizable as the dreadlocked puli. Its corded coat was originally developed to protect the dog from the brutal winters of the Hungarian plains, where it herded sheep. These days, it's more for show. In fact, the puli's coat, which naturally cords, can be brushed out or clipped short. Whichever hairstyle the dog gets, it will be the same pup underneath: a faithful friend that's remarkably agile and a quick learner. With the puli, mental activity is as important as physical, and the dog should be challenged to keep it from just doing whatever it wants.

Pyrenean Shepherd

🏅 **Tireless Herder**

AKC Breed Popularity No. 181
Temperament Affectionate, active, enthusiastic **Average Size** 15–21 inches, 15–30 pounds **Activity Level** Average **Shedding** Seasonal **Trainability** Agreeable **Life Expectancy** 15–17 years

Pyrenean Shepherd

As a hard-working herder in the mountains on the border of France and Spain, the Pyrenean shepherd would cover as much as 25 miles a day—and sometimes, only two dogs managed 1,000 sheep. Hundreds of years later, the breed remains alert and lively, and requires mental and physical activities to channel that energy and keep the dog balanced. Whip-smart and trainable, the Pyrenean shepherd (which comes in rough- and smooth-faced varieties) loves games and intense activity, making it a great candidate for pretty much any canine sport, especially agility, obedience, dock diving and freestyle work.

Rat Terrier

Rat Terrier
🎖 **Calm and Cool**
AKC Breed Popularity No. 86
Temperament Friendly, inquisitive, lovable **Average Size** 10-13 inches (miniature) 13-18 inches (standard), 10-25 pounds **Activity Level** Average **Shedding** Seasonal **Trainability** Easy **Life Expectancy** 12-18 years

As its name describes, the rat terrier was originally bred to exterminate rodents. Yet when off-duty, it was also trained to protect the family and play with children—two jobs the breed still takes seriously today. Whether it's of the miniature or standard variety, the happy-go-lucky rat terrier is a tough little dog and tends to do best with other canines of the same size or larger. The calmest of the terriers, the rat terrier is still high-energy and requires daily exercise in the form of playing indoors with a human companion or chasing a ball around a fenced-in yard. So long as the rat terrier is with its family, it's happy and healthy.

Redbone Coonhound
🎖 **Handsome Hunter**
AKC Breed Popularity No. 142
Temperament Even-tempered, amiable, eager to please **Average Size** 21-27 inches, 45-70 pounds **Activity Level** Average **Shedding** Seasonal **Trainability** Easy **Life Expectancy** 12-15 years

A quintessential coonhound, the redbone is an expert at balancing vigorous activity with rest (after all, its prey—raccoons—is nocturnal). But even more so, it's recognized for its flashy red coat, the result of selective breeding to ensure good looks. The redbone is an incredible athlete and especially sure-footed on any terrain, making it an ideal workout buddy (always on-leash) for joggers, bikers or hikers. At home though, the breed is a mellow and loyal family dog.

Redbone Coonhound

Rhodesian Ridgeback
🎖 **Renaissance Hound**
AKC Breed Popularity No. 41
Temperament Affectionate, even-tempered **Average Size** 24-27 inches, 70-85 pounds **Activity Level** Average **Shedding** Seasonal **Trainability** Agreeable **Life Expectancy** 10-12 years

Named for the stripe of backward-growing hair along its back, the breed can pretty much do it all. Originally bred to track (but not kill) lions, the Rhodesian ridgeback was also noted for its devotion to family and tolerance for children—which remain today. Although not chasing lions these days, the dog does still have a strong prey drive and should never be allowed off-leash unless in a secured area. Similarly, never turn your back on them in the kitchen: The ridgeback is a notorious "counter surfer" and will help itself to any food left out unattended.

Rhodesian Ridgeback

8th MOST POPULAR BREED!

Rottweiler
🏅 **Best People Dog**
AKC Breed Popularity No. 8
Temperament Loyal, loving, confident guardian **Average Size** 22-27 inches, 80-135 pounds **Activity Level** Average **Shedding** Occasional **Trainability** Agreeable **Life Expectancy** 9-10 years

The picture of power, the Rottweiler is a robust dog with a gentle side that's devoted entirely to its cherished family. As strangers will learn, the breed is aloof and confident, making them especially imposing and an ideal watchdog. With its loved ones though, the Rottweiler is playful and silly—and will even try to climb up in your lap for a cuddle! Because it loves its humans so much and can be territorial about them, early basic training and socialization, beginning in puppyhood, is an absolute must. Although the breed is highly intelligent and trainable (Rottweilers were one of the first to be guides for the blind), it can be stubborn, so remain consistent and firm. Another important thing to remember: Avoid roughhousing, as it could encourage aggression.

Russell Terrier
🏅 **Little Entertainer**
AKC Breed Popularity No. 82
Temperament Alert, inquisitive, lively
Average Size 10-12 inches, 9-15 pounds
Activity Level Energetic **Shedding** Occasional **Trainability** Agreeable
Life Expectancy 12-14 years

Look can be deceiving with the Russell terrier: Although the breed resembles a stuffed toy dog, it's as tough as it is cute and cuddly. Bred to hunt foxes in England, it's a tireless and inquisitive worker that won't let up until the job is complete. Because of this disposition, the breed does require quite a bit of daily activity to burn off all its energy, whether it's going for long walks or hikes or running alongside its human owner for a jog or bike ride. At home though, the Russell terrier is a jaunty little fellow with a big personality that loves to entertain its family with tricks—and with its high intelligence, the possibilities are endless when it comes to what tricks it can learn!

Russell Terrier

S

Saint Bernard

Saint Bernard
🏅 **Genial Giant**
AKC Breed Popularity No. 48
Temperament Playful, charming, inquisitive **Average Size** 26-30 inches, 120-180 pounds **Activity Level** Average **Shedding** Seasonal **Trainability** Agreeable
Life Expectancy 8-10 years

One of the few breeds considered "nanny dogs," the Saint Bernard is famous for its unbridled patience, devotion and loyalty when it comes its family, especially the littlest members. Although it has a natural instinct to be protective, the dog doesn't realize it's so massive and powerful, meaning early obedience classes and socialization are crucial. The Saint Bernard needs to be trained not to jump up on people, especially small children, and inadvertently knock them down. Fortunately, the breed is so kindhearted and eager to please, it will learn good behaviors quickly. Despite its large size, the Saint Bernard, which comes in long- and short-hair varieties, doesn't require vigorous exercise. One long walk or a 30-minute play session in the yard daily should be enough to keep the lovable pup healthy and happy.

Saluki

Saluki
🏅 **Most Independent**

AKC Breed Popularity No. 120 **Temperament** Gentle, dignified, independent-minded **Average Size** 23-28 inches or smaller, 40-65 pounds **Activity Level** Energetic **Shedding** Occasional **Trainability** Independent **Life Expectancy** 10-17 years

It's no wonder the Saluki is considered Egypt's royal dog. Its beauty is something to behold: sleek and leggy with a dignified expression framed by long feathered ears. A dog of this magnificence does require special attention, though. With the breed's instinctive independence, obedience training is a necessity. The sight hound should also receive regular daily exercise—and it must always be on a leash or secured in a well fenced-in yard away from traffic, as the Saluki is a notorious escape artist.

Samoyed
🏅 **Best Cuddler**

AKC Breed Popularity No. 59 **Temperament** Adaptable, friendly, gentle **Average Size** 19-23.5 inches, 35-65 pounds **Activity Level** Energetic **Shedding** Seasonal **Trainability** Independent **Life Expectancy** 12-14 years

One look at the smiley Samoyed, and it's impossible not to beam

Samoyed

back. The breed's hallmark expression is actually practical: The corners of its mouth are upturned to keep the dog from drooling, thus preventing icicles from forming on its face—a necessary feature during its origins as a sled dog in Siberia. Another ancient instinct is its need to be bonded to humans—it used to huddle with the Samoyedic people for warmth—and it's vital that the modern dog enjoy activities with its family or it will be mischievous and act out. And with the Samoyed's strong urge to run off and roam, that's an ill-fated combination.

Schipperke
🏅 **Little Captain**

AKC Breed Popularity No. 105 **Temperament** Confident, alert, curious **Average Size** 10-13 inches, 10-16 pounds **Activity Level** Average **Shedding** Seasonal **Trainability** Independent **Life Expectancy** 12-14 years

The schipperke's name, "Little Captain" in Dutch, says it all. In its Belgian homeland, the dog earned its keep as an exterminator on ships and a guardian of dockyards. Although small, the robust breed is built for a big job, with its powerful jaw, neck and forequarters. Inherently, it's very active and needs daily exercise to be balanced. The playful and curious schipperke loves exploring, be it in a fenced-in

Scottish Deerhound

Schipperke

yard or around a small home. Because of this instinct, early training is needed to teach the dog to come when called.

Scottish Deerhound
🏅 **Tallest Breed**

AKC Breed Popularity No. 158 **Temperament** Gentle, dignified, polite **Average Size** 28-32 inches, 75-110 pounds **Activity Level** Average **Shedding** Seasonal **Trainability** Independent **Life Expectancy** 8-11 years

The rare Scottish deerhound is a majestic creature known as the Royal Dog of Scotland. Originally bred to stalk 400-pound red deer, all these centuries later, it demands daily free runs (in a securely fenced play area) to be physically and mentally healthy. And although adult dogs can become couch potatoes, regular exercise must be maintained. Scottish deerhounds, especially puppies, benefit from a canine playmate and are ideal for families who enjoy a household with more than one dog.

Shetland Sheepdog

Scottish Terrier

Scottish Terrier
🏅 **Most Persistent**
AKC Breed Popularity No. 57
Temperament Confident, independent, spirited **Average Size** 10 inches, 18-22 pounds **Activity Level** Average **Shedding** Occasional **Trainability** Independent **Life Expectancy** 12 years

The Scottish terrier's spirit is as beloved as its comical wiry beard. With an almost humanlike personality, the breed is bold, clever and independent-minded (which can make training a challenge). The dog is also high-energy and persistent—which explains its nickname, The Diehard. So brisk walks and fun activities, such as chasing a ball or playing tug-of-war with its favorite toy, are necessary. But that doesn't mean the Scottish terrier requires a yard: The breed actually does very well in small homes or apartments...but not always around other dogs.

Sealyham Terrier
🏅 **Strongest Small Breed**
AKC Breed Popularity No. 164
Temperament Alert, outgoing, sense of humor **Average Size** 10.5 inches, 23-24 pounds **Activity Level** Average **Shedding** Seasonal **Trainability** Independent **Life Expectancy** 12-14 years

Sealyham Terrier

Not quite big enough to be considered a medium-size dog, the Sealyham terrier's muscled build and outgoing personality makes it the strongest of the small breeds—and it has the big-dog bark to match. And with its sly sense of humor and affectionate nature, the Sealyham is also one of the most delightful. Whether in the city or suburbs, the adaptable breed is right at home. It enjoys regular exercise, but special attention must be paid when the dog is outside: Not only will it overheat in a humid climate, but its predominantly white coat is prone to grass stains, so be prepared to invest in pet wipes in addition to bathing it every few weeks.

> **DID YOU KNOW?**
> The most famous show dog during Prohibition was a Sealyham terrier named Bootlegger.

Shetland Sheepdog
🏅 **Most Obedient**
AKC Breed Popularity No. 25
Temperament Playful, energetic, bright **Average Size** 13-16 inches, 15-25 pounds **Activity Level** Average **Shedding** Seasonal **Trainability** Eager to please **Life Expectancy** 12-14 years

Similar to its bigger cousin, the collie, the Shetland sheepdog is also bright, obedient and agile, all qualities that make it a superstar in canine sports. At home, the Sheltie is an affectionate pet and alert watchdog. Whether it lives in the city or suburbs, it's vital that the herding breed always be walked on a leash or allowed to play in a well-fenced yard, since it will chase any moving thing, including cars. A quirk of the Sheltie is barking unnecessarily, a behavior that can be curbed with training (they are quite biddable).

Shiba Inu
🏅 **Housebreaking Champ**
AKC Breed Popularity No. 44 **Temperament** Alert, active, attentive **Average Size** 13.5-16.5 inches, 17-23 pounds **Activity Level** Average **Shedding** Seasonal **Trainability** Independent **Life Expectancy** 13-16 years

The oldest and smallest of the Japanese breeds, the shiba inu is the No. 1 companion dog in its home country. And over the past 50 years, its popularity has grown in the U.S. as Westerners have discovered the dog's good-natured temperament and excellent housebreaking instincts. By 4 weeks of age, a puppy will get far away from its sleeping area to eliminate. By 5 weeks, it will hold it all night, until

Shiba Inu

Shih Tzu

Silky Terrier

Siberian Husky

it's taken outside. Energetic but not hyper, the shiba inu is content with daily walks—but the breed can never, ever be allowed off-leash unless in a secured area. No amount of training can prevent the dog from bolting the moment it sees an escape.

Shih Tzu
🏅 Master Manipulator

AKC Breed Popularity No. 20 **Temperament** Affectionate, playful, outgoing **Average Size** 9-10.5 inches, 9-16 pounds **Activity Level** Average **Shedding** Infrequent **Trainability** Agreeable **Life Expectancy** 10-18 years

For hundreds of years, the shih tzu was the pampered lapdog of Chinese royalty. These days, the breed (believed to be the product of crossing a Lhasa apso and a Pekingese) still treats its owners like kings and queens. Bred to be a prized house companion, the modern shih tzu is equally content to play indoors, with brief outings for fresh air and potty breaks, making it a perfect pet for apartment dwellers, including those with children. The amusing little dog with the long, flowing coat is undeniably cute—and most of them know it. The shih tzu has a tendency to use looks and charm to manipulate humans into letting it have its way, which is why basic training is important, albeit frustrating. Owners must

be firm, using methods based on praise and reward, and not give in when the dog misbehaves (now matter how cute its antics may seem). And, naturally, with a coat this stunning, maintenance is necessary. In addition to daily brushing (including its mustache), the corners of the eyes should be cleaned. The profuse hair on the dog's head can irritate its eyes and should be trimmed or tied up into a bun. Don't have time to dedicate to its demanding beauty routine? A groomer can give it a short "puppy cut," which is just as adorable.

Siberian Husky
🏅 Most Beautiful Eyes

AKC Breed Popularity No. 12 **Temperament** Loyal, outgoing, mischievous **Average Size** 20-23.5 inches, 35-60 pounds **Activity Level** Energetic **Shedding** Seasonal **Trainability** Independent **Life Expectancy** 12-14 years

The legendary sled dog will draw you in with its almond-shaped eyes (which can be brown or blue—or one of each), but will keep you with its friendly demeanor. Despite its connection to snowy climates, the Siberian husky can thrive anywhere, as long as the pack breed has pals. "Siberians are generally happy, outgoing dogs who love to

be around people and other dogs," explains Sandy Weaver, education coordinator for the Siberian Husky Club of America. "They like the companionship of another animal— they do best in twos, threes or more." For the energetic and smart husky, activity should be mental in addition to physical. "Walks, runs, trotting alongside a bike are great ways to burn off some of their energy," says Weaver. "Playing hide-and-seek, where the dog uses his dominant sensory channel—his nose—to find the hidden object is also great fun for them."

Silky Terrier
🏅 Atypical Lapdog

AKC Breed Popularity No. 112 **Temperament** Friendly, quick, keenly alert **Average Size** 9-10 inches, around 10 pounds **Activity Level** Average **Shedding** Occasional **Trainability** Agreeable **Life Expectancy** 13-15 years

Slightly larger than the Yorkshire, the silky terrier is similar in temperament (charming and feisty), build (sturdy) and silky coat (feels like human hair)—but it's certainly not your average lapdog. The bold breed requires more exercise than most toy pups and even loves a game of fetch. The silky also adapts to any living situation, because as long as it has its human, it's a happy dog.

Sloughi

Smooth Fox Terrier

Skye Terrier

Skye Terrier
♀ Cutest Ears
AKC Breed Popularity No. 178 **Temperament** Brave, good-tempered **Average Size** 10 inches, 35-45 pounds or less **Activity Level** Calm **Shedding** Seasonal **Trainability** Independent **Life Expectancy** 12-14 years

Considered one of the AKC's most distinctive-looking breeds, the Skye terrier is twice as long as it is tall, with a peekaboo hairdo and big, feathery ears that stand up like bat wings. And its laid-back personality is just as pleasing: The breed has minimal exercise needs and is satisfied with whatever lifestyle its human companion chooses—although it does enjoy canine sports, like agility and Earthdog (underground hunting) events, if given the opportunity. The Skye terrier is reserved by nature, so early socialization is recommended to ensure an outgoing pet.

> **DID YOU KNOW?**
> Skye terriers got popular in the 19th century, when Queen Victoria inspired a fad with British women.

Sloughi
♀ Shy Soul
AKC Breed Popularity No. 192 **Temperament** Reserved, graceful, aristocratic **Average Size** 24-29 inches, 35-50 pounds **Activity Level** Energetic **Shedding** Infrequent **Trainability** Independent **Life Expectancy** 10-15 years

Nicknamed the Arabian Greyhound because of its origins hunting jackals, gazelles and wild pigs in the desert, the sloughi is physically very similar, with an elegant yet robust body. The breed's big dark eyes, often described as "melancholy," reflect its shy and aloof demeanor, especially around strangers. At home with its loved ones, the sloughi is gentle and sedate— but get it outside for a full-out run (in an enclosed area, of course), and it's a whole new animal! The breed also excels at canine sports, especially lure coursing, where it can really show off its natural sight-hound skills.

Smooth Fox Terrier
♀ Little Daredevil
AKC Breed Popularity No. 123 **Temperament** Friendly, independent, amusing **Average Size** 15.5 inches, 15-18 pounds **Activity Level** Energetic **Shedding** Occasional **Trainability** Agreeable **Life Expectancy** 12-15 years

More than 200 years ago, the smooth fox terrier was developed to assist in fox hunts, its sole job being to harass the prey until it bolted from its hole. And all these generations later, the breed (which is quite similar to its cousin, the wire fox terrier) still has the reputation of a lively and athletic little dog that enjoys the chase— although these days it sticks to tennis balls. Another instinct that's hardwired is digging, so owners with meticulously manicured yards will need to teach the dog otherwise. Whether living in the suburbs or city, the alert smooth fox terrier will make an excellent watchdog without being aggressive.

Soft-Coated Wheaten Terrier
♀ Merry Extrovert
AKC Breed Popularity No. 53 **Temperament** Friendly, happy, deeply devoted **Average Size** 17-19 inches, 30-40 pounds **Activity Level** Energetic **Shedding** Infrequent **Trainability** Independent **Life Expectancy** 12-14 years

The soft-coated wheaten terrier is the essence of a happy dog, from its

Spinone
Italiano

Staffordshire
Bull Terrier

peekaboo hairdo and goatee to its friendly temperament. Originally bred as an Irish farm dog, it's retained much of the high energy—which won't diminish even in old age, so owners should expect many years of daily exercise with their exuberant pet. While smart, the soft-coated wheaten is very stubborn and can have its own agenda, making early obedience training and firm discipline a must before the dog matures and its bad habits stick.

Spanish Water Dog
♛ Curly-Coated Charmer
AKC Breed Popularity No. 153
Temperament Playful, work-oriented, upbeat **Average Size** 15.75-19.75 inches, 31-49 pounds **Activity Level** Energetic
Shedding Infrequent **Trainability** Eager to please
Life Expectancy 12-14 years

A dual-purpose breed used as a herder and waterfowl retriever, the Spanish water dog is an inexhaustible worker that knows when to relax. While they enjoy vigorous exercise, puppies should refrain from it until they've reached full maturity and their bone-growth plates have closed. Then they can safely accompany their humans on adventures, like running, hiking and, of course, swimming. The loyal charmer—its curly coat should never be brushed—is wary of strangers, so early socialization is essential.

Spinone Italiano
♛ Sensitive Sweetie
AKC Breed Popularity No. 109
Temperament Sociable, patient, docile
Average Size 22-27 inches, 64-86 pounds **Activity Level** Energetic
Shedding Regularly
Trainability Agreeable
Life Expectancy 10-12 years

Famed for its versatility as a hunter on land and in water, there are lots of reasons to love the spinone Italiano. Sociable and intelligent, it's been gaining popularity in the U.S. Although built for endurance, it moves slower than other pointing breeds. The sensitive pup responds well to positive reinforcement. Don't count on him as a watchdog—the spinone barely barks.

Staffordshire Bull Terrier
♛ True Blue
AKC Breed Popularity No. 80
Temperament Clever, brave, tenacious **Average Size** 14-16 inches, 24-38 pounds **Activity Level** Energetic **Shedding** Occasional
Trainability May be stubborn
Life Expectancy 12-14 years

Just one spot behind its cousin the American Staffordshire terrier in popularity, the Staffordshire bull terrier is also a powerful dog that has evolved from a fighter to become a trustworthy family pet with a reputation for being patient with children. But while sweet and loyal with people, the breed's strong prey drive can remain, making early obedience training and socialization imperative to ensure that your Staffie is on its best behavior around other canines. Fortunately, with its intellect and desire to please, training should be pretty smooth.

Soft-Coated
Wheaten Terrier

Spanish
Water Dog

Standard
Schnauzer

Swedish
Vallhund

Sussex Spaniel
🏅 **Slow-But-Steady**
AKC Breed Popularity No. 180
Temperament Friendly, merry, even-tempered **Average Size** 13-15 inches, 35-45 pounds **Activity Level** Average **Shedding** Seasonal Trainability Independent
Life Expectancy 13-15 years

Despite its frowning expression, the Sussex spaniel has a cheerful disposition. "Slow but steady" best describes the breed, whether it's hunting birds or relaxing at home. Similarly, its body also grows at a rate that's not as quick as that of other dogs. Puppies should avoid strenuous exercise until at least a year old. By the time it reaches 18 months, the dog can safely enjoy swimming, jumping and agility-type activity.

Swedish Vallhund
🏅 **Most Balanced**
AKC Breed Popularity No. 169
Temperament Friendly, active, watchful **Average Size** 11.5-13.75 inches, 20-35 pounds **Activity Level** Energetic **Shedding** Seasonal **Trainability** Eager to please **Life Expectancy** 12-15 years

Another breed that once sailed with Vikings, the long and low Swedish vallhund is believed to be the offspring of Scandinavian spitzes mixed with Welsh corgis. The herder's sturdy little body is the picture of balance and power, with a no-frills, dense coat that needs only an occasional bath and brush. Although it has boundless energy, not all dogs of the breed require the same level of activity to channel it. For the most part, one good walk a day (plus a game of fetch) should fill the bill.

Standard Schnauzer
🏅 **Most Reliable**
AKC Breed Popularity No. 89
Temperament Friendly, alert, happy
Average Size 17.5-19.5 inches, 35-50 pounds **Activity Level** Average **Shedding** Infrequent
Trainability Independent
Life Expectancy 13-16 years

Right in between the very popular miniature and much-bigger giant versions, the medium-size standard schnauzer sits in a class all its own. The energetic breed does everything with passion, whether that's being a sociable companion, excelling at obedience training or even just romping around in the backyard. Ever-reliable, the standard schnauzer is also a protective watchdog and especially great with children. Because the breed loves its family so much, it's best to involve the dog in your daily activities whenever possible.

DID YOU KNOW?
Standard schnauzers were utilized by the German army as dispatch carriers and Red Cross aides.

Sussex
Spaniel

Tibetan Mastiff

Tibetan Mastiff

T

Tibetan Spaniel

food, and it sometimes skips meals altogether. But allow the dog to get bored, and it'll acquire a sudden appetite for wood—with your furniture being the snack

Tibetan Mastiff
🏵 **Loyal and Aloof**
AKC Breed Popularity No. 131
Temperament Independent, reserved, intelligent **Average Size** 24-26 inches minimum, 70-150 pounds **Activity Level** Average **Shedding** Seasonal **Trainability** Independent **Life Expectancy** 10-12 years

According to natives of the breed's homeland, Tibetan mastiffs possess souls of monks and nuns not yet ready to be reincarnated into people, so that tells you a lot about its temperament: calm and wise. For such a powerful dog, it needs only moderate activity and especially loves work-related exercise, like playing catch or patrolling the property. The breed tends to reserve its energy, with only bursts of liveliness, although it's more active in cooler weather. Contrary to two misconceptions about the massive and abundantly furry Tibetan mastiff, it doesn't shed or eat much

Tibetan Spaniel
🏵 **Most Agreeable**
AKC Breed Popularity No. 119
Temperament Playful, bright, self-confident **Average Size** 10 inches, 9-15 pounds **Activity Level** Calm **Shedding** Seasonal **Trainability** Agreeable **Life Expectancy** 12-15 years

Exponentially smaller than the Tibetan mastiff, the Tibetan spaniel originally worked in tandem with its cousin as a Buddhist monastery watchdog: While the mastiff acted as the brawn, the spaniel was the eyes and would scan the horizon for both friends and foes. Off-duty, they were loving companions— and to this day, the breed worships the ground on which its owner walks. Due to its calm demeanor, a daily walk is just fine for the Tibetan spaniel, although it can certainly keep up on a jog, if its human desires. And if its cherished family prefers to relax indoors instead, the dog is just as happy to accommodate them with that as well.

DID YOU KNOW?
Female Tibetan mastiffs go into heat only once a year, in the fall, so puppies are born in the winter.

Best Guard Dogs

A family dog can be both loving pet and intimidating protector. Several breeds are able to tap into their natural instincts when a stranger arrives at the home or if it senses a threat to its family. The AKC lists these breeds as the best guardians based on size, fearlessness and loyalty.

Belgian Laekenois

Bullmastiff

Doberman Pinscher

German Shepherd Dog

Giant Schnauzer

Rottweiler

Staffordshire Bull Terrier

Tibetan Mastiff

175

YOUR PERFECT MATCH

Toy Fox Terrier

Treeing Walking Coonhound

Tibetan Terrier
🏆 **Most Holy**

AKC Breed Popularity No. 96
Temperament Affectionate, loyal, sensitive **Average Size** 14-17 inches, 18-30 pounds or slightly smaller **Activity Level** Energetic **Shedding** Seasonal **Trainability** Independent **Life Expectancy** 15-16 years

The third breed in the Tibetan trifecta, the Tibetan terrier is revered as the "Holy Dog" (and a symbol of luck) in its homeland, where it also served as a watchdog and companion. Similar in appearance to its cousin, the Lhasa apso, the Tibetan terrier tends to be more loving and energetic and especially enjoys being outdoors with its family (although some individual dogs can have a lower drive for exercise). Still, the breed's instinct to act as a sentinel indoors persists, and it's important for the dog to have its own "post" where it can look out a window or glass door. (Bonus points if the perch is in a higher position, like a stair landing or balcony).

Toy Fox Terrier
🏆 **Tiny and Terrific**

AKC Breed Popularity No. 111
Temperament Friendly, alert, intelligent **Average Size** 8.5-11.5 inches, 4-9 pounds **Activity Level** Energetic **Shedding** Occasional **Trainability** Eager to please **Life Expectancy** 13-15 years

The toy fox terrier is a toy breed through and through. Developed by mixing smooth fox terrier runts with miniature pinschers, Italian greyhounds and Chihuahuas, it possesses the amusing charm to match. It also has plenty of qualities that reflect its terrier side—primarily tenacity—and is also big on intelligence, courage and love for its family. An extrovert that loves to please, the breed is easy to housebreak, whether it's training the dog to relieve itself outside or inside, on a designated potty pad, making it ideal for apartment living. The toy fox terrier does love the outdoors though—especially running around the yard or enjoying a walk.

Treeing Walker Coonhound
🏆 **People's Choice**

AKC Breed Popularity No. 137
Temperament Smart, brave, courteous
Average Size 20-27 inches, 50-70 pounds **Activity Level** Average **Shedding** Seasonal **Trainability** Independent **Life Expectancy** 12-13 years

With its brave-yet-sensible temperament as a hunter, devotion to family and sweet face, it's no wonder the treeing walker coonhound is nicknamed The People's Choice. Although bred in the mid-18th century to "tree" prey, meaning to follow the scent until the creature scurries up a tree for safety and keep it there for human hunters, walkers love to run. And the dog's high energy must be burned off with regular exercise, making it the perfect workout buddy for joggers or hikers (just be sure the dog always remains on-leash). At home though, the low-maintenance breed loves nothing more than to curl on the sofa with its human companion.

V

Vizsla
🏆 **Versatile Athlete**

AKC Breed Popularity No. 31
Temperament Affectionate, gentle, lively **Average Size** 21-24 inches, 44-60 pounds **Activity Level** Energetic **Shedding** Seasonal **Trainability** Eager to please **Life Expectancy** 12-14 years

Vizsla

The pride of Hungary, the vizsla has steadily become more popular with Americans since it was smuggled out of the then-Communist country back in the 1950s. Still today, the breed is beloved for its stunning golden-rust coat, loving temperament and tight bond with humans. Because of its origins as a versatile gun dog with strong stamina, it requires at least 30 minutes a day of exercise. The vizsla is athletic and eager to get outside, so an active owner looking for a jogging or biking companion would be the most ideal. The dog is highly intelligent and curious and will need consistent training, starting as a puppy, to channel its energy.

Weimaraner
Q Perfect Hunter
AKC Breed Popularity No. 36
Temperament Friendly, fearless, obedient **Average Size** 23-27 inches, 55-90 pounds **Activity Level** Energetic **Shedding** Seasonal **Trainability** Eager to please **Life Expectancy** 10-13 years

Bred as the perfect hunting dog, the Weimaraner has done it all—

from pursuing bears and lions to pointing and retrieving game. The breed was such a secret in Germany, it didn't arrive in the U.S. until the 1920s. These days, hunters and pet owners alike cherish its friendliness, obedience and smarts. It's also excellent with kids and is happiest when treated as a family member.

Welsh Springer Spaniel
Q Happy and Handsome
AKC Breed Popularity No. 128
Temperament Happy, reserved, upbeat **Average Size** 17-19 inches, 35-55 pounds **Activity Level** Energetic **Shedding** Regular **Trainability** Easy **Life Expectancy** 12-15 years

Stronger than the cocker spaniel yet smaller than the English springer spaniel, the Welsh springer spaniel is a medium-size dog revered for its happy disposition and eye-catching red-and-white coat. Although a versatile hunter on all terrains, at home, the breed (one of Britain's oldest spaniels, dating back to 250 B.C.) is a devoted companion,

especially for those with an active lifestyle. The Welshie is energetic and most content when it's playing with its family in the yard or enjoying a long walk with its owner.

Welsh Terrier
Q Calmest Terrier
AKC Breed Popularity No. 107
Temperament Friendly, intelligent **Average Size** 15 inches or smaller, 20 pounds **Activity Level** Energetic **Shedding** Occasional **Trainability** Agreeable **Life Expectancy** 12-15 years

One of the more calm terriers in the canine world, the Welsh terrier is still quite spirited—after all, its original job, hundreds of years ago, was to dig badgers out of their lairs. The breed should be provided with lots of time to run in an enclosed area, in addition to daily long walks, to burn off energy and be well-behaved. While friendly, the Welsh terrier does need to be adequately socialized with other dogs as a puppy to ensure it's polite when encountering other canine friends.

Weimaraner

Welsh Springer Spaniel

Welsh Terrier

West Highland White Terrier

West Highland White Terrier
♀ **Endlessly Entertaining**
AKC Breed Popularity No. 42
Temperament Loyal, happy, entertaining **Average Size** 10-11 inches, 15-20 pounds **Activity Level** Average **Shedding** Seasonal **Trainability** Agreeable **Life Expectancy** 13-15 years

For more than 300 years, the West Highland white terrier has been a cherished companion, beloved for its charm, cleverness and spunk. Although a little white dog, it's a sturdy breed that loves to romp around in the yard—just be sure it's fenced-in, since the Westie was bred to hunt rats and will instinctively chase after anything that moves. The Westie's irresistible coat, which is not as soft and fluffy as it appears, does require regular grooming to look its best. In addition to doing daily brushing, the dog should be taken to a professional every four to six weeks. It should also be noted that bathing a Westie too often can actually do more harm than good to its hard double coat.

Whippet
♀ **Gentle Soul**
AKC Breed Popularity No. 61
Temperament Affectionate, playful, calm **Average Size** 18-22 inches, 25-40 pounds **Activity Level** Average **Shedding** Occasional **Trainability** Independent **Life Expectancy** 12–15 years

Whippet

The most popular of the greyhounds, the whippet falls in between the other two: It's nearly three times the size of the toy Italian greyhound, yet it's smaller and not as fast as the greyhound (although at 35 mph, the whippet is no slowpoke). Calm in the home, the natural sprinter comes alive once outside on a free-run or retrieving session—just be sure off-leash adventures always take place in a fenced-in area. Because the whippet preserves its energy at rest, the sweet breed is ideal for those who live in apartments but don't want a small dog, so long as the whippet receives adequate daily exercise, of course.

DID YOU KNOW?
Since 1953, the bloat is mostly white with no red so it's not mistaken for a fox during a hunt.

Wire Fox Terrier
♀ **Natural Comedian**
AKC Breed Popularity No. 101
Temperament Confident, alert, gregarious **Average Size** 15.5 inches, 15-18 pounds **Activity Level** Average **Shedding** Infrequent **Trainability** Agreeable **Life Expectancy** 12-15 years

Just as its name describes, the wire fox terrier was originally developed as a hunter with a coarse coat, back in the late 1700s in England. But over time, the charming breed has evolved into an amusing companion

Wire Fox Terrier

Wirehaired Pointing Griffon

and award-winning entertainer, with a record 13 Westminster Kennel Club Best in Show titles. Training the wire fox terrier can be challenging, as it bores easily, but with patience and consistent, fun sessions, it's certainly achievable. Still, never allow even the best-trained wire fox terrier off-leash in an unsecured area—all it has learned will be overshadowed by natural instinct the moment it spots any small animal that it views as prey.

Wirehaired Pointing Griffon
♀ **Supreme Gun Dog**
AKC Breed Popularity No. 65
Temperament Friendly, devoted, trainable **Average Size** 20-24 inches, 35-70 pounds **Activity Level** Energetic **Shedding** Seasonal **Trainability** Agreeable **Life Expectancy** 12-15 years

There's no other gun dog like the wirehaired pointing griffon. Out on the field, it's versatile and tireless in pursuit of everything from upland birds and waterfowl to furred game. Similarly at home, the breed, which is characterized by a rugged appearance, is just as devoted to being a pleasant pet. Social and energetic, the wirehaired pointing griffon is best suited for active families who include their dog in daily routines. If its mental, physical and emotional needs are not met, it will definitely become unhappy and, possibly, destructive.

Wirehaired Vizsla
Q Ideal Workout Buddy
AKC Breed Popularity No. 167
Temperament Gentle, loyal, trainable
Average Size 21.5-25 inches, 45-65 pounds **Activity Level** Energetic
Shedding Seasonal
Trainability Agreeable **Life Expectancy** 12-14 years

Similar in temperament and versatility to the vizsla, the slightly taller wirehaired vizsla is its own distinct breed distinguished by a course coat and shaggy beard. Just like its sleek cousin, the breed is high-energy and requires lots of exercise. Since the wirehaired vizsla is happiest when doing something with its family, a good idea is to combine the two and bring the dog, while secured on a leash, along for a jog, hike or bike ride. Back at home though, it is calm and gentle.

Wirehaired Vizsla

Xoloitzcuintli

Xoloitzcuintli
Q Quiet Protector
AKC Breed Popularity No. 140
Temperament Loyal, alert, calm
Average Size 10-14 inches, 10-15 pounds (toy); 14-18 inches, 15-30 pounds (miniature); 18-23 inches, 30-55 pounds (standard) **Activity Level** Energetic **Shedding** Infrequent
Trainability Agreeable
Life Expectancy 13-18 years

Possibly the hardest to pronounce, the Xoloitzcuintli ("show-low-eats-QUEENT-lee") has been a national treasure of Mexico for 3,000 years. Xolos come in a variety of sizes and coat types: toy, miniature and standard and either hairless or with a short, flat coat. The hairless version is ideal for those with allergies (just be sure to protect the dog's skin with sunscreen). Although an alert dog, don't expect your Xolo to do much barking.

Yorkshire Terrier

Yorkshire Terrier
Q Big Personality
AKC Breed Popularity No. 10
Temperament Affectionate, sprightly, tomboyish **Average Size** 7-8 inches, 7 pounds **Activity Level** Average
Shedding Infrequent
Trainability May be stubborn
Life Expectancy 11-15 years

Looks can be deceiving with the Yorkshire terrier. Beneath its floor-length silky coat is a sturdy dog with a feisty disposition. That confident attitude, along with its charming personality and unending devotion for its human, is why the breed often tops most-popular lists in various big American cities. Although it's one of the tiniest breeds, the Yorkie doesn't know that. The dog carries itself like a big dog and considers itself a formidable protector of its family. It certainly doesn't require the physical activity of one—but the Yorkie does enjoy twice-daily walks at a steady pace and the occasional game of fetch. As for the Yorkie's trademark silky coat, it's hypoallergenic and rarely sheds. Very similar to human hair, it does require some maintenance though: If kept long, it should be brushed daily.

DESIGNER DOGS

What do you get when you cross two purebreds?
An expensive mutt with a tongue twister of a name—but a face
that's easy to love.

Labradoodle, Maltipoo, goldador, puggle, bassetoodle, Chiweenie, Morkie—no, these aren't characters from a Harry Potter novel. Over the past three decades, pairs of pure breeds have been crossed to create brand-new mixed breeds. But don't dare call them mutts: Designer dogs, as they're referred to, are considered purebred by those who love them, although purists in the canine community disagree.

The first designer dog was developed in the late 1980s, when a blind woman in need of a guide dog requested one that didn't shed, because her husband was allergic. Wally Conron, the puppy-breeding manager for the Royal Guide Dog Association of Australia, set out to find a dog that fit the tall order. Since the standard poodle is known to be a worker, Conron focused on

training the nonshedding breed. "I tried 33 dogs in the course of three years, and they all failed," he explained in an interview with Stanley Coren, PhD. "They just didn't make the grade as guide dogs." On a whim, he crossed his best female Labrador retriever with a standard poodle, which created three puppies. But because they weren't purebred, no foster families were interested in caring for them (which typically includes training and socializing) until they were old enough to enter the guide-dog program.

"I went to our PR team and said, 'Go to the press and tell them we've invented a new dog, the Labradoodle,'" recalled Conron. "It worked—during the weeks that followed, our switchboard was inundated with calls from potential dog-fostering homes, other guide-dog centers, vision-impaired people and people allergic to dog hair

SCHNOODLE

Schnauzer + Poodle

Temperament Charming, smart, alert
Average Size 10-12 inches, 10-20 pounds
Life Expectancy 13-17 years

Two of the most alert pure breeds create one excellent (and adorable) little watchdog. Still, the schnoodle loves to get out of the house for daily walks or playtime and is rather adaptable to its human's lifestyle. If given the opportunity to participate in canine sports, such as agility, obedience or fly ball, the dog will excel. The schnoodle—which is typically the result of a mini schnauzer and poodle—can have a wiry or curly coat and a sturdy or slender build, depending on which of the two breeds is more dominant.

Designer breeds get their name because they were invented, or "designed," by the people who love them.

who wanted to know more about this 'wonder dog.'" But as Conron soon discovered, while adorably irresistible, as the combination of two distinct breeds, the Labradoodle didn't possess predictable traits like a pure breed would. In the first litter, all three puppies' coats tested as nonallergenic. Yet in the second, only three of the 10 pups had the same results. Although it's not a big deal for owners who simply love the look and temperament of the Labradoodle, it is for those who suffer from allergies.

Thirty years later, there are as many as 500 varieties of designer dogs—ranging from a mix of popular breeds, like the goldendoodle (golden retriever + poodle) and Yorkiepoo (Yorkshire terrier + poodle), to the more obscure Puggit (pug + Italian greyhound) and Sharmatian (Shar-Pei + Dalmatian). The trendiest designer dogs are typically half-poodle or half-golden, due to their reputations for being highly intelligent. Although most fans of designer dogs insist the hybrid is truly the best of both worlds, purebred preservationists think otherwise. "We support responsible breeding to help improve the health and longevity of the breed while preserving its temperament and original function," says Amanda Brumley, a breeder with Waterfront Golden Retrievers in Richmond, Kentucky. "With a purebred dog, there is a predictability of the outcome of future generations, which is not always the case with outcrossing."

While careful breeding can certainly produce designer dogs with the most desirable traits from each breed, genetics are always uncertain. Sometimes they can be enhanced, resulting in increased health or longer life spans. Other times, recessive undesirable traits can end up dominating. "For example, standard poodles, goldens and Labs all share the problem of hip dysplasia," explains Susan Burge, president of Poodle Club of America. "Mini and toy poodles share the same genetic makeup as cocker spaniels for progressive retinal atrophy," meaning a crossbreeding of the two could potentially be risky.

That's why it's important when selecting a designer dog to do proper research and find a responsible breeder, preferably one who genetically tests their stock—just as you would with a pure breed.

> ## Although the AKC doesn't recognize designer dogs, it does allow them to participate in events.

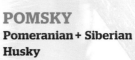

POMSKY

Pomeranian + Siberian Husky

Temperament
Smart, agile, fun

Average Size
10-15 inches, 7-38 pounds

Life Expectancy
12-15 years

Two unlikely breeds come together to produce, arguably, one of the cutest puppies in the canine world. Because of its parentage (which is typically the result of artificial insemination, due to the vast difference in size of the pure breeds), the dog is available in a wide range of colors, including gray/white, brown/red, blue merle and blonde, with a soft coat and fluffy tail. While the Pomsky can vary in size, it makes for a fun playmate for children—although not ideal for those too young to understand the need to be gentle with such a little dog.

GOLDADOR

Golden Retriever + Labrador Retriever

Temperament Social, smart, energetic **Average Size** 22–24 inches, 60–80 pounds **Life Expectancy** 10–15 years

A cross between two of the most popular family dogs, the Goldador is an equally beloved member of the household, especially noted for its good-natured temperament with both kids and other pets. Other pluses for the Goldador (or Glab, as it's also known): It's one of the healthier designer dogs and so easygoing that it's a good choice for first-time owners. Also, as one of the larger designer hybrids, it's an easily trainable athlete, making the Goldador a go-to guide, search-and-rescue and drug-detection dog.

Interested in a designer dog but don't want to purchase from a breeder? Adopt a pup from a rescue!

COCKAPOO

Cocker Spaniel + Poodle

Temperament
Happy, loving, charming
Average Size
height varies, 10–30 pounds
Life Expectancy
14–18 years

There are so many variables with the cockapoo, no two puppies in a litter may look or behave the same—with coats anywhere from sleek to curly in an array of colors, such as black, white, tan, red, brown, silver and brindle. Whatever the combination, it should be low-shedding, yet it will require extensive brushing to prevent matting. Although an individual cockapoo's temperament depends on which parent it inherits it from, typically it's a sweet, people-oriented dog that can easily adapt to living in a big home in the suburbs, or in the city.

CAVAPOO

Cavalier King Charles Spaniel + Poodle

Temperament
Fun-loving, outgoing, sweet
Average Size height varies, 12–25 pounds
Life Expectancy
10–15 years

Also known as the Cavoodle, the Cavapoo is an exceptional companion dog, no matter what you call it. Friendly and loving, it's perfectly content to curl up in its owner's lap—or enjoy some indoor play time. With its moderate activity level, diminutive size and high adaptability, the Cavapoo, whose coat can be curly or straight, is an especially ideal pet for apartment dwellers who don't have much space.

◀ GOLDENDOODLE
Golden Retriever + Poodle

Temperament Affectionate, gentle, loyal

Average Size 13–20 inches, 15–35 pounds (miniature); 17–20 inches, 40–50 pounds (small standard); 20–24 inches, 50–90 pounds (large standard)

Life Expectancy
10-15 Years

The goldendoodle is a wonderful companion to everyone in the home, including children and other dogs. Although it can vary in size from miniature to large (depending on whether the golden was bred with a toy, miniature or standard poodle), the goldendoodle is typically very playful and loves a yard to run around in—although an apartment will do with proper exercise. With the golden's high trainability and the poodle's supreme intelligence, the crossbreed is a great candidate to work as a service dog.

◀ LABRADOODLE
Labrador Retriever + Poodle

Temperament Intelligent, friendly, intuitive

Average Size 14-16 inches, 15-25 pounds (miniature); 18-20 inches, 30-45 pounds (medium); 22-24 inches, 45-65 pounds (standard)

Life Expectancy
10-15 Years

Widely considered hypoallergenic, the hybrid is one of the most popular designer dogs today. Because of the unpredictability of genetics, its coat can be anywhere from wiry to soft and straight, wavy or curly. Although it's not guaranteed that every Labradoodle won't shed, it does so less than a purebred Labrador. Like the goldendoodle, it typically comes in a variety of sizes and coat colors, depending on its poodle parentage. This makes the Labradoodle an ideal choice whether you would prefer a small, medium or large dog. No matter the size, it promises to be a loving, kid-friendly family pet. 🐾

Labradoodles come in a variety of colors, including chocolate, apricot, black and silver.

SPECIAL THANKS TO CONTRIBUTING WRITERS:

Leslie Barrie, Jillian Blume, Janet Lee, Megan McMorris, Gail O'Connor, Brittany Risher, Katherine Schreiber, Alyssa Shaffer, Celia Shatzman

CENTENNIAL BOOKS

An Imprint of
Centennial Media, LLC
40 Worth St., 10th Floor
New York, NY 10013, U.S.A.

ISBN 978-1-951274-16-0

Distributed by
Simon & Schuster, Inc.
1230 Avenue of the Americas
New York, NY 10020, U.S.A.

For information about custom editions, special sales and premium and corporate purchases,
please contact Centennial Media at contact@centennialmedia.com.

Manufactured in China

Publishers & Co-Founders Ben Harris, Sebastian Raatz
Editorial Director Annabel Vered
Creative Director Jessica Power
Executive Editor Janet Giovanelli
Deputy Editor Alyssa Shaffer
Design Director Ben Margherita
Senior Art Director Laurene Chavez
Art Directors Natali Suasnavas, Joseph Ulatowski
Production Manager Paul Rodina
Production Assistant Alyssa Swiderski
Editorial Assistant Tiana Schippa
Sales & Marketing Jeremy Nurnberg